Together Let Us Sweetly Live

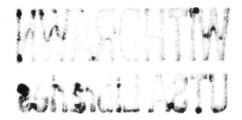

Music in American Life

A list of books in the series appears at the end of this book.

Together Let Us Sweetly Live

THE SINGING AND PRAYING BANDS

Jonathan C. David

with photographs by Richard Holloway

UNIVERSITY OF ILLINOIS PRESS

URBANA AND CHICAGO

Publication of this volume was supported by a grant from the
Maryland State Arts Council, an agency funded by the State of
Maryland and the National Endowment for the Arts.

∞ This book is printed on acid-free paper.

Library of Congress Cataloging-in-Publication Data
Together let us sweetly live : the singing and praying bands /
[interviews compiled and edited by] Jonathan C. David,
with photographs by Richard Holloway.
p.   cm. — (Music in American life)
Includes bibliographical references and index.
ISBN-13: 978-0-252-03170-0 (cloth : alk. paper)
ISBN-10: 0-252-03170-9 (cloth : alk. paper)
ISBN-13: 978-0-252-07419-6 (pbk. : alk. paper)
ISBN-10: 0-252-07419-x (pbk. : alk. paper)
1. Church music—Methodist Church—Maryland.
2. African American Methodists—Maryland—Interviews.
3. Camp meetings—Maryland. I. David, Jonathan C.
ML3170.T64   2007
781.71'760089960730752 1—dc22   2006100927

Together let us sweetly live,
Together let us die;
And each a starry crown receive,
And reign above the sky.

—A wandering verse used by the Singing and Praying Bands to conclude the old hymn "Blest Be the Tie That Binds," by John Fawcett (1740–1817). This verse originally derives from the hymn "Jesus, Great Shepherd of the Sheep," by Charles Wesley (1707 88). Since the nineteenth century, it has been popular as a camp-meeting chorus.

Contents

Hymn Notations

Preface

IN THE SUMMER OF 1983, I was hired by the Delmarva Folklife Festival to scour three counties of northeastern Maryland in search of folk artists, musicians, storytellers, and the like. My fieldwork began when an employee of the Maryland Legal Services office in Centerville, Maryland, introduced me to a relative of hers who was an African American seafood wholesaler on Kent Island. He in turn put me in touch with black watermen working in the creeks off the Eastern Shore of the Chesapeake. One summer day when I was out on the water with a waterman with the wonderful name of Baby Jack Lynch, I inquired about musical traditions on Kent Island or in its vicinity. I forget Mr. Lynch's exact words, but he began by saying something like, "If you go over to the church in Batt's Neck during their camp meeting, you'll hear these people come and sing this really old-time type of singing. And the melodies are so slow and strange that you won't understand a word they say."

A "neck," incidentally, is Chesapeake-area talk for a peninsula of land that juts out into the bay. Batt's Neck is a small African American community on the west side of Kent Island.

Lynch continued, "And outside of the church and down the road a hundred yards or so will be a group of people drinking and carrying on."

Lynch steered the boat back and forth along a half-mile crab line, snatching the crabs one by one off the line, setting them onto a large table in the rear of the boat to separate the jimmies (the mature males) from the females, and throwing the peelers (the young crabs) back into the tepid waters of the bay. As he trolled along, Lynch suggested that I talk to a particular man in Batt's Neck named Pete Bordley. He would know about this kind of singing, he said.

I went to the poor but highly civilized community of Batt's Neck, south of Stevensville, just south of the east terminus of the Chesapeake Bay Bridge, and knocked on Bordley's door.

Bordley answered the door and listened to my request politely, but he told me that he knew little personally about these old singing groups, called Singing and Praying Bands. (Group members always capitalize the name of their organization, and I will follow their lead.) Instead, he directed me to his neighbor's house, saying that the resident there, Rev. Edward Johnson, was very knowledgeable on the subject.

I thought I was getting the runaround, but I knocked on Rev. Johnson's door just the same. Johnson, who was the organizer of his church's camp meeting, asked me inside, invited me to attend the camp meeting at Batt's Neck, and welcomed me back time and again. This despite his wife's initial fear that I was trying to sell them life insurance.

When I first heard the Singing and Praying Bands at the camp meeting in Batt's Neck's Ezion United Methodist Church, I did not, as the waterman predicted, understand many of the words they sang. The hymn tunes were also unlike anything I had ever heard. But it was obvious that the service and the singing were *good*. *Really* good. And I knew that anything that good was bound to have a great deal of passion—as well as a good story—underlying it.

After the summer job had been completed, I kept returning to different churches to see the Singing and Praying Bands as they traveled from church to church and from camp meeting to camp meeting. Gradually, this fieldwork turned into a larger project, and that larger project turned into the focus of my longer-term research.

I began research about the Singing and Praying Bands against the advice of almost everyone to whom I mentioned my plans, including most of the professors I knew in the Department of Folklore and Folklife at the University of Pennsylvania. Their argument made a great deal of sense. I had, after all, no apparent academic background in African American studies. Furthermore, the legacy of racism in America is so immense that one cannot naively rush into a project such as this; years of preparation are usually preferable.

Yet I pushed ahead despite the potential for race and class conflict. A middle-class white man is tolerated when he walks into a black church in the rural South, it seems to me, in part because the people in the pews of such churches do not generally have the social power to exclude him, if indeed that is what some might want. A black man entering a white church in traditional areas of the rural South most likely would not be given the same charitable welcome that I received. My position in the churches of the Singing and Praying Bands was to some degree an inherently culturally imperialist one; I have no illusions about this dynamic.

Yet the more my friends and acquaintances warned me against proceeding, the more I felt that this was a project that had chosen me to undertake it. It was not merely that the Singing and Praying Bands were, well, absolutely dynamite. When I sat down and talked about the bands with band members, the stories of the folk culture out of which they grew—the church pageants, the yard art, the trickster stories, the stories of magic, of spectral phenomena, of oyster tonging, and so on—seemed so rich as to be irresistible. There is an argument in the United States today that black people ought to be empowered to tell their own stories to others rather than have others tell their stories for them. Without delving into the subtle pros and cons of this argument, I can say that in general I agree with it. Yet I persisted with this project. I risked the cultural imperialism, because I had faith in the potentially positive outcome for both the bands and for me. I decided to trust myself, and to trust the rapport that I built with the individuals in these groups, at first with Rev. Edward Johnson of Batt's Neck, and then with many others in the bands.

I had been planning for years to do research in India. I was indeed prepared—perhaps overly prepared—for that eventuality. Yet just before the time came to fly off to the other side of the world, my mother died a difficult death of ALS. My whole family was thrown for a loop. Today, I am much more familiar with the geography of death. But that was my first intimate experience with human mortality; at the time, I took it hard. Under no conditions could I take myself off to India as if nothing had happened. By then, I had been working with the Singing and Praying Bands for two years. When the trip to India was called off, I moved this project from the back to the front burner.

I have never had a particular academic axe to grind in writing about the Singing and Praying Bands, not when I began, not now. My overriding interest in the bands has always consisted in the fact that I find their religious practice to be profound and moving. At the time I began my research, I was coming out of my own lifelong experience of depression and psychological devastation, an experience that I thought of as my own private holocaust. Entering into my first camp meeting at Ezion United Methodist Church in Batt's Neck on Kent Island, Maryland, I was stunned by the manner in which members of the bands—and particularly their ancestors—had created a whole and meaningful universe for themselves out of the holocaust of slavery and Jim Crow, by creating with each other and for themselves a social, musical, and spiritual reality from scratch each time they got together. They could have just as easily, perhaps more easily, chosen nihilism. Choosing life is more brave.

Somehow, my decision not to pursue research in India heightened my awareness of myself as an American. The work with the bands offered me a focus on two major factors that have shaped American culture, and therefore shaped me: first, the legacy of slavery that continues to distort all of American society, and second, the tremendous influence that evangelical Christianity has had on the American consciousness. Finally, my work following the Singing and Praying Bands to a different church in a different part of the Chesapeake Bay area of America every week gave the restless wanderer within me the opportunity to live out, in a restricted but nevertheless real way, my late twentieth-century, thoroughly American, Kerouacian fantasies.

Previously, I have written about the Singing and Praying Bands in a completely academic voice. Yet that academic voice did not seem adequate for a book that sought to describe the soulfulness of the prayer band phenomenon. We all complain when we are made to read dry analytical tomes in which the inherent fascination of the "stuff" of folk cultures is lost. I decided to attempt to overcome this obliteration of the folk soul. In 1996, when one of my friends in the Singing and Praying Bands died of prostate cancer, I swung into action. I began to put together a book of oral histories based on the ethnographic interviews that I had conducted with numerous individuals. While each individual maintains her or his voice in the present book, all of the questions that an ethnographer would ask of an informant are answered unobtrusively.

In the first chapter, for example, Alfred Green explains to a reader exactly what a camp meeting is, what a Singing and Praying Band is, what a mourners' bench is, and how the whole camp-meeting event proceeded, beginning to end. In the second chapter, Mary Allen outlines for a reader what an entire Singing and Praying Band service would look and sound like. In chapter 3, Samuel Jerry Colbert explains how hymns are raised, while in chapter 4, Gertrude Stanley speaks about how one composes a prayer. Rev. Edward Johnson speaks in chapter 5 of the patterns of reciprocity in work and social life that formed the backbone of social interactions in the African American town in which he grew up. He explains how the ways that the older generation had of helping each other carried over into the Singing and Praying Bands, and into the bands' own networks of reciprocity. He adds that the spiritual apotheosis of these traditions of mutual aid was the shout, which band members tended to experience together. In the sixth chapter, Cordonsal Walters also explains in great detail traditions of reciprocity in the work lives of his parents and grandparents, as they labored as sharecroppers on land that other people owned. He also speaks about the intricacies of the shout as a dance step, or more properly, as a "motion." Further, he speaks about the origin and oral tradition of the two-line narrative verses that band members often add to the choruses with which they conclude a service. In chapter 7, Susanna Watkins speaks about the evolution of camp meetings when they became an urban phenomenon, as country folks moved into the city of Baltimore. Further, she describes the uniforms band members wore, and the events at which the bands performed—such as watch night service on New Year's Eve—other than camp meetings. She also speaks of how the Singing and Praying Bands' aesthetic of call-and-response grew out of the traditions of mutual aid and cooperation—a tradition that they simply call "help"—underlying African American social life of that time and place. In chapter 8, Benjamin Harrison Beckett and George Washington Beckett address the issue of how the Singing and Praying Band service and the camp meetings in general grew out of a society in which each town was made up of interrelated extended families. The brothers also speak at length about the folk architecture of the camp-meeting tents that they and their family and friends built on the campground at Antioch A.M.E. in Frankford, Delaware. Finally, Gus Bivens adds the voice of a folk poet to the book, describing cryptically how he composed narrative couplets to be added to choruses that the bands call "straight hymns," and how new hymns sometimes came to him as he was drifting off to sleep. He also echoes the sentiment of many contemporary band members, that the bands of today are but a pale reflection of those of the past, in the commitment of their members and in their spiritual power. Intertwined with this exposition on the history and ethnography of the bands are stories that offer a window into the lives of individuals who made up the bands, who *were*, and still *are*, in fact, the bands.

Folklorists and oral historians recognize the dilemma that hounds the researcher who undertakes a long trek to interview an informant, hoping to return with eloquent direct quotations to include in the text on which he or she is working. All too frequently one comes home to transcribe those thoughtful, moving words of the interviewee, only to discover that the tape recordings are full of "ums" and "ers" and sentence fragments, dangling participles, and unanswered questions. An interviewer often forgets to ask the questions that in hindsight seem to be most crucial. Given the dilemma posed by fragmented answers and unasked questions, I began writing this book by asking myself how I could develop an honest process of editing individuals' accounts of their own experiences and refining the raw material of these interviews into coherent narratives, while eschewing manipulation of the interviewees' words.

Though I undertook this process with difficulty, I did develop my own technique. I began with one advantage. I had, as mentioned previously, written an earlier, briefer work on the same subject, and I had interviewed a few of the same individuals whom I interviewed for this book. From the very beginning of this project, then, I did not have to struggle to understand the tradition on which I was focusing. Instead, I knew in advance to whom I would go to ask about the various important aspects of the tradition. I knew for example, that Alfred Green, as captain of the band at the church with the largest camp meeting, would be the best person to interview about the basic questions a reader would need to know to understand the tradition: What is a camp meeting? What is a Singing and Praying Band? What is a mourners' bench? I interviewed Cordonsal Walters because I knew in advance that he could explain the shout as a set of motions and steps. I interviewed Mary Allen because I knew she could explain with eloquence and detail the progress of a band service from beginning to end. I had the luxury of asking familiar questions about familiar subjects of individuals with whom I was already on friendly terms, in order to record their presentation of the truths of this tradition in their own words.

I began my editing process by interviewing the same individual several times, often asking the same questions in successive interviews and recording the individual's responses several times. In this way, I would ensure that I had accurately understood each story or each interpretation of tradition. I also strove to ensure that each retelling was consistent with previous accounts. After transcribing the initial interview, I would return for a second and third interview with the same individual and flesh out the interviewee's responses to my initial questions with more detailed questions, eliciting more descriptive elaboration.

After I had interviewed one of the band members two, three, or four times, and after I had transcribed these interviews, I began to think about how to edit the words of the interviewee, how to edit each sentence, how to tell each story, and how to build a sequence of stories into a narrative that flows well from beginning to end. When starting, I recalled the words of the esteemed folklorist Kenny Goldstein.

Goldstein remarked on many occasions—for reasons that I did not understand at the time—that in conversation, no one ever ends one sentence and begins another. A long recorded monologue from the same individual may actually be a single utterance, one independent clause after another, strung together with "ands" and "and thens" and "buts." Similarly, no one speaks in completely formed paragraphs. When a folklorist commits these words to writing, adding periods, commas, and paragraph breaks, she or he inevitably revises the spoken word. In transcribing an informant's words we change them. This change is inevitable and acceptable.

Using Goldstein's observations as a starting point, I came to a more general conclusion about the nature of spontaneous speech: the spoken word often consists of provisional declarations. Speakers almost inevitably hesitate, go back, restate, shift their emphases, change their minds, and change their words, in the midst of a single utterance. If an interviewee's own words are provisional, I decided, a folklorist who commits these words to writing need not treat their initial order as if they are inviolable.

Furthermore, the order of the stories or detailed explanations that an interviewee provides is largely random. In the initial stages of an interview, the interviewee's presentation of details follows the order of the researcher's questions, which may not follow any particular order. In later stages of an interview, the interviewee may take over and begin explaining aspects of the tradition that she or he finds to be important, answering questions a researcher did not have the prescience to ask. At moments during an interview, conversation between interviewer and interviewee may simply flow spontaneously. Since the presentation of detail in an interview does not follow a linear order, the writer or editor may put these details into a narrative order, as I have done here.

Keeping these precepts in mind, I tentatively began the process of boiling down the raw material of the interviews into the refined product of the final narratives presented here. In the sixty, seventy, or eighty pages of interview text from a single individual, I had, as previously mentioned, recorded multiple versions of interviewee answers to the same question. The transcripts contained plenty—in fact more than enough—of elaboration, idea development, and detail for each point.

From the separate interviews, I searched out several descriptions of the same subject; I excerpted these passages from the various interview transcripts and wrote them out together in one place, each different telling of the same story perhaps adding a new detail. In editing Alfred Green's recollections of the camp meetings at Magothy, I excerpted his various accounts of his conversion experience and his several descriptions of collecting lightwood stumps and what fire stands looked like; how vendors sold food, snake oil, or what have you to those in attendance on the campgrounds; how different bands would sing on the church grounds at the same time; how drinkers and gamblers gathered there; and how a man made money there playing three-card monte. Then I placed similar accounts together on one page.

At that point, I began to edit the descriptive paragraphs on lightwood and fire stands, using the same techniques I use when I teach college students how to edit their own writing: move this sentence here; make that dependent clause part of the next sentence; invert the next sentence so that the independent clause comes first; put these clauses into a sequence and make verbs parallel in structure for emphasis; find the most important sentence and move it to the beginning to be the topic sentence of the entire paragraph. When a narrator told a story using direct quotations to convey the words of the story's protagonists, I would retain grammatical constructions of black vernacular English. Otherwise, I translated each and every sentence into Standard English, as I believe that individuals in the band wanted me to do.

At the same time that I separated out details of the many rich descriptions and distinct stories— how the cook tents were spread out, the way the captain would blow the horn to announce the beginning of a new service, and so on—I began to formulate a sequence for the unfolding of the narrative as a whole. Alfred Green, for example, told me on several occasions the story of how he was converted to Christianity as an adolescent. In fact, Green told everyone about his conversion experience, almost never failing to recount it when he was asked to lead a testimony service while visiting another band captain's camp meeting or band day. I decided that that story was of such merit that it deserved to occupy the first page of the first chapter of the book as a whole. I did not make this decision from my own personal wisdom. Albert Raboteau, the venerable historian of religion, once gave me a charge to attend to individuals' accounts of their own conversion. Raboteau's advice and Green's eloquence convinced me to begin here.

After this story, I placed the paragraphs I had culled from Green's words answering my questions "What is a camp meeting?" and "What is the purpose of a camp meeting?" From that moment in the chapter onward, almost every sentence of Green's story is an answer to a direct question that I posed. Although I already knew many of the answers myself, I was determined to prompt Green to describe the events, the terms, the pictures, the sounds to an outsider. After he described what a camp meeting is, I asked him to tell me what prayer meetings are and what Singing and Praying Bands are, who the leaders are, who the leaders of his church's band were in the past, and so on. Sometimes I broke each question down into several smaller questions to ensure the answers would make sense to an audience of outsiders. When Green had a story to tell, I would sit back in my seat and listen quietly to his intrinsic eloquence about memories of special concern to him. I would find a place to insert that story among his descriptions of the details of a camp meeting.

I concluded Green's chapter with his account of the events of final mornings of the camp meetings at his home church. At the moment of fashioning Green's complete narrative, in one of those magical moments that happen to writers all too infrequently, I was struck as if by a bolt of lightning with two realizations. First, I saw that while originally I had been most interested in Green's conversion as a story that would stand alone, his conversion happened at the conclusion of the camp meeting that he had just described. Second, I realized that the text of the transcribed interviews contained other accounts of the same story that I had not used at the beginning of the chapter. That shorter version fit well at the chapter's conclusion. Whereas at first I was interested in the conversion story in and of itself, in the end I had found that this story was embedded within the larger story of the camp meeting tradition as a whole. The result of this editing was what I hope readers find to be engaging storytelling.

While some will undoubtedly question aspects of my editing techniques, the results seem to me to be valid. Rather than reading each person's testimony in this book as a primary, unfiltered source, readers should see these narratives as portraits that I, the folklorist, painted, using the informant's own words and stories. These portraits do indeed resemble the speakers; individuals to whom I read their chapters recognized themselves, their stories. Yet the portraits also bear as much of the unmistakable technique of the writer as a painting bears the brushstroke of the painter.

I took ancestral stories from the oral tradition at face value. A formally trained historian, I suspect, might doubt the objective truth of Cordonsal Walters's story of his grandmother with which chapter 6 opens. Yet a folklorist recognizes that family stories, while sometimes acquiring the stuff of legend, have a truth of their own that must be attended to. Absolute truth is unobtainable. Had the bands been blessed with different researcher, a different book would have resulted.

What emerges from this approach is a descriptive, hopefully somewhat artful portrait of a religious folk-song service and the folk culture out of which it arose, along with the patterns of folklife lived by the many individuals who brought it into being. I asked Richard Holloway if he would chronicle the bands on film; his photographs accompany the texts of these individual stories. With extensive help from Eugene Montague, a musician and musicologist, I transcribed into musical notation some of the bands' repertoire. I set to work on an introduction that would frame the personal narratives that form the body of the book, while also reconnecting today's Singing and Praying Band members with the distant past in Africa and early America that has been almost lost to the oral tradition. In the introduction, I also present an argument about the bands' larger importance in the history of African American and American culture.

I believe that truth is simple but seldom seen. I hope that the simplicity of this book will not be mistaken for simplemindedness, but as informing a conceptual depth. I hope the loving work that has emerged from my efforts, while simple and modest, will engage readers intellectually, emotionally, and spiritually. I hope that readers will allow themselves to be transported, even if only partially and momentarily, to a place from which they may be able to view the world through the eyes of—and feel the world with hearts of—members of the Singing and Praying Bands.

There are many people I would like to thank for their help in the preparation of this book. These include Roger Abrahams, Albert Raboteau, David Hufford, and Don Yoder, at the University of Pennsylvania; my crack music transcriber, Eugene Montague; my brilliant photographer, Richard Holloway, his photographically accomplished wife, Tanya, and their patient children, Caroline and Robin; my professional colleagues and friends Phyllis Solomon, Jeffrey Draine, Charles Bergengren, Glenn Hinson, Greg Jenkins, Sally Peterson, Orlando Rideout V, and Polly Stewart; and my great personal friends Steven E. Taylor, Ellen Slack, Jerry Colbert, and Joyce Pressley.

I thank those at the Delmarva Folklife Festival for hiring me twenty years ago, and staff of the American Folklife Center for lending me recording equipment. Over the years, the Philadelphia Folksong Society, the Folk Arts Division of the National Endowment for the Arts, the Maryland Historical Trust, the Maryland Humanities Council, the William G. Baker Foundation, the Anne Arundel County Arts Council, and the Delaware Division of Parks and Recreation enabled this project to move along by providing funding.

The Reverends Irving Lockman, Bernard Keels, Wallace L. Greene Sr., Robert Brown, Edward Jackson, John Milton Harvin, Calvin Price, Albert Giles, Webster Whittington, and Jeremiah Lee, along with Rev. Ronald Ward of Asbury Town Neck and Rev. Louis Shockley of Christ United Methodist in Baltimore and others, allowed me to record in their churches.

Many members of the Singing and Praying Bands donated their time and their expertise to this project. Susanna Watkins, Alfred Green, Bernard White, Mary Allen, Jerry Colbert, Gertrude Stanley, George Beckett, Benjamin and Mildred Beckett, Cordonsal Walters and Elizabeth Hall, Gus Bivens, James Cromwell, Keiford Jackson, Charles Raymond Stanley, Sherman and Florence Wilson, George Meekins, and Ralph and Viola Opher all shared their time with me and my intrusive tape recorder. Ruth and Charlie Stanley, Leona Spicer, Cliff and Hazel Williams, Catherine Ennels, Nettie Kane, Juanita McDonald, Bubby Dorsey, Gladys Stanley, Enez Stafford-Grubb, Malchi Wheately, Lilly Chester, Roosevelt and Maggie Cornish, Oscar Johnson, Joseph Louis Parker, Mary Randall, Wilton Jennings, Harrison Tindley, Ruth Watkins, Elva Tongue, Anthony Johnson, and Carrie Smith have all helped me along. I will never forget any of them. Others whose photos or songs appear in this book have been an inspiration.

Rev. Edward Johnson of Batt's Neck welcomed me into his home, his church, and his church's camp meetings. He spent many hours patiently explaining the Singing and Praying Bands to me, and explaining my presence to other members of the bands. Without his hospitality and his knowledge, this work could never have been accomplished.

All these members of the Singing and Praying Bands shared songs and stories with me on condition that no use, reuse, or commercial use would be made of the material except with my permission.

My father, William M. David Jr., attended many camp meetings with me after the death of my mother, and he contributed a photograph to this book. This companionship was very special for both of us. He became a friend of many of the members of the Singing and Praying Bands, and his presence thereby gave me a family context with which to relate to band members. With my father present, I became a neighbor and friend who, to some extent, willingly shared my life with them as they, to some extent, did with me. It is to my father, may he rest in peace, that I dedicate this book. These precious memories linger.

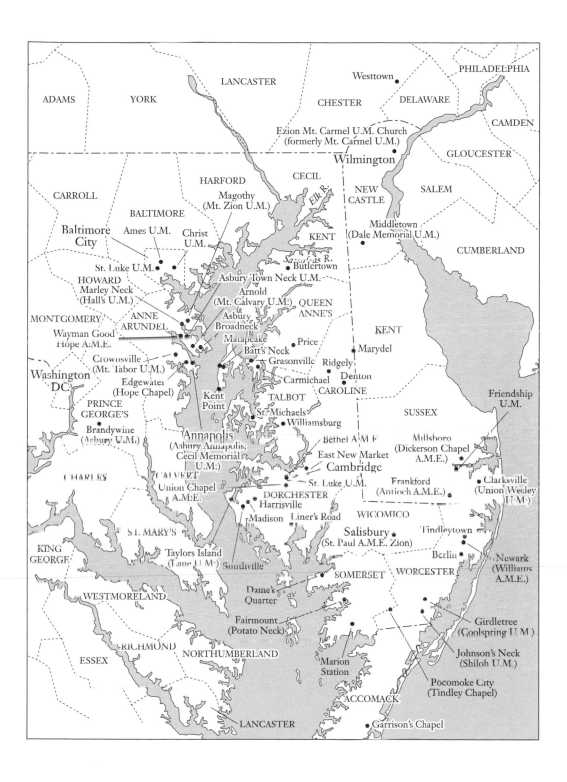

Together Let Us Sweetly Live

Introduction

IN THE EARLY YEARS of the twentieth century, according to the older people of today, many African American residents of tidewater Maryland and Delaware would, in late summer, set aside their tools, leave their cornfields just when the tassels on each stalk turned golden and the tips of each blade changed from green to brown, abandon their tomatoes when a soft blush of red appeared on the hard green fruit, allow, for a time, their beans and sweet potatoes and melons to mature on their own, and make their way by horse and wagon, by car, or by bus to a Methodist camp meeting to attend to their sacred work.[1] Those who had moved to the nearby cities of Baltimore, Wilmington, or Philadelphia in search of the higher wages and the excitement that urban life seemed to offer returned home by land or by water, traveling perhaps on one of the ferries that plied the Chesapeake or Delaware bays from city to town, from shore to shore, and back again.[2]

If the camp meeting was nearby, some individuals, families, or groups of unrelated church members might attend nightly services and return home to sleep, to work the next day perhaps, but then steadfastly to make their way right back to that same camp meeting for the next night's service, and the next, until that camp meeting's final, cathartic day.[3] During several of the old-time country camp meetings, however, many would unhitch their horses, arrange all the separate wagons into a circle around a wooden-roofed tabernacle, arch a sheet of canvas over each wagon, and stay right there on the church ground for the duration of the meeting. Women would bring baskets and cheese boxes filled to the brim with fried chicken, home smoked ham, biscuits, cabbage, and green beans.[4] Men and boys would dig up old pine stumps and pile them high on the campgrounds, to be placed on fire stands and set ablaze to give light to each evening's spectacle.[5] In the heat of the summer, when the ground might be parched and dust might billow—when you couldn't even walk across the ground barefoot, it was so hot—everyone lived in the shade, and "everyone had a *good* time," as one person recounted later.[6] For two weeks, an intense but relaxed, joyful, communal "laboring in the Spirit" manifested itself in a day-after-day pattern of an exuberant testimony service, followed by a rousing preaching service, followed at last by a climactic, regionally distinct Singing and Praying Band service. During this latter service, in a maneuver that scholars might refer to as a "ring shout," participants formed a circle with a leader in the center; singing and clapping their hands, stamping their feet, and swaying their bodies all the while, they slowly "raised" several hymns and spirituals to a raucous, rejoicing, shouting crescendo, concluding the meeting with an ebullient march around the entire encampment.[7] Although these bands shocked some outsiders and reminded other observers of Africa,[8] committed participants considered them to be the foundation of the church.

Camp meetings were not unique to this area or to that time at the dawn of the twentieth century. Drawn by the heady combination of religious salvation and spiritual democracy advocated in these festivals, Americans of various backgrounds had been making such yearly treks to camp meetings for over a hundred years.[9] Those early meetings gave form to a religious movement attuned to the ethos of the new nation. In the frontier areas of Tennessee and Kentucky where they began, camp meetings sponsored by various Protestant denominations became temporary sacred cities, places of equality of souls and social solidarity that tempered the struggle to survive in the wilderness. In the states of the upper South and in Pennsylvania, these meetings also thrived. Here, where the camp meetings were predominantly organized by Methodists, both free and enslaved African Americans participated in large numbers along with English- and German-speaking European Americans.[10] Perhaps because of Methodism's original antislavery witness, in Maryland, for example, this denomination received most of the black converts, while in 1800, approximately one-fifth of the Methodists in Virginia were black.[11]

At the beginning of the nineteenth century, white and black people alike frequently attended the same religious services, though often in segregated and unequal seating arrangements. Yet that century witnessed a complex and powerful movement to establish separate religious institutions for black Methodists. First came the effort to set up separate churches for Africans. Eventually the Methodist Episcopal Church organized a separate conference for all black churches within its denomination.[12] A related movement led to the founding of independent, African Methodist denominations. Finally, beginning before Emancipation but accelerating after freedom, a similar but less-remarked effort saw African American Methodists starting camp meetings of their own. In the mid-Atlantic region in particular, these large, outdoor, African American religious events were the meetings that the grandparents and great-grandparents of today's participants built and today's older people witnessed when young. These camp meetings continue even in the twenty-first century.

The camp meetings that the old soldiers of today recall were not unique; they were merely one echo of the religious festivals that became a new secular democracy's first religious mass movement. Yet the old-timers of today recall, above all other things, those aspects of their camps that *were* unique. That is, they speak mostly about the Singing and Praying Bands, for whom the camp meetings in this area became the primary regional showcases; *these* bands made *these* meetings special. They tell of the prayer meetings from which the camp meetings originated. They speak also of the march around Jericho, in which the Singing and Praying Bands led those at the camp meeting in a grand march around the entire campground on the final day of the meeting.

The Singing and Praying Bands of this area were special not just for the generations of participants in the African American camp meetings of the Atlantic coast states of the upper South. The antecedents of the twentieth-century bands seem to have played a clandestine but significant role in the development of African American culture in general. Therefore, the bands can stake a claim as important forces in the cultural and social history of America as a whole.

Here is how it happened. At the end of the eighteenth century, when enslaved Africans in this area began to take to Methodism in a big way, the process of culture building by which Africans of various ethnic backgrounds began to transform themselves into one people was well underway. Yet that process was still incomplete. The new African American identity became consolidated throughout the South only during the first half of the nineteenth century, when hundreds of thousands of enslaved Africans were traumatically sold from the states of the upper South to cotton-growing areas of the Deep South.[13]

In the eighteenth century, prior to this mass transfer of human property, there had been two primary centers of slavery on the Atlantic coast of North America: coastal South Carolina and the Chesapeake Bay area. The ethnic mix of Africans imported into the two areas differed somewhat, leading to the possibility that the emerging African American cultures of these areas might also have differed. Of these two centers, the Chesapeake area had the larger number of slaves.[14] In 1790, of all thirteen states, Virginia had the largest population of Africans, with 305,493 people. Maryland was second, with 111,079. Virginia also had the largest number of enslaved Africans—292,627—while Maryland's enslaved population of 103,036 was third largest. These two states also had the largest population of non-slave Africans at the time. In 1790, nearly 53 percent of the African population and 58 percent of the enslaved Africans in the country were in the upper South, in the states of Virginia, Maryland, and Delaware.[15] The nearby black populations of southeastern Pennsylvania and southwestern New Jersey had extensive cultural ties to their brethren in the upper South.

This area where the upper South meets the mid-Atlantic states seems to have been one of several areas central to the formation of African American culture in the late eighteenth and early nineteenth centuries. Among the Africans in America of that time, for example, those who lived in the mid-Atlantic region and upper South were pioneers in building specifically black institutions. In 1787, Richard Allen, Absalom Jones, and others founded a mutual aid organization in Philadelphia called the Free African Society, initiating, in the words of W. E. B. DuBois, "the first wavering step of a people toward organized social life."[16] Numerous other grassroots benevolent and mutual aid organizations sprouted up at this time, aiming to provide members financial assistance in case of sickness or death in the family.[17] Under the leadership of Richard Allen in Philadelphia, a group of black Methodists established the Bethel African Church in that city in 1794.[18] In 1816, Bethel joined ranks with other independent black Methodist churches in Pennsylvania, New Jersey, and Baltimore to form the African Methodist Episcopal (A.M.E.) denomination. In Wilmington, the denomination called the Union Church of Africans was established just prior to the founding of the A.M.E. Church.[19]

Along with new institutions, a distinctly African American expressive culture was emerging in the upper South and mid-Atlantic region at the dawn of the nineteenth century. In 1819, for example, a white minister named John Fanning Watson, who lambasted many Methodists for what he saw as excesses in their worship, gave us one of the earliest reports of a specifically black religious song tradition, writing that "the coloured people get together, and sing for hours together, short scraps of disjointed affirmations, pledges, or prayers, lengthened out with long repetition choruses."[20] In the same paragraph, Watson's description of these sacred performances by black worshippers is strikingly evocative of outdoor singing circles that the Singing and Praying Bands continue to this day. This account predates by over twenty-five years the earliest known description of a ring shout from the Atlantic coast area of the Deep South.[21] Another writer, a Quaker schoolboy from Westtown School outside Philadelphia, described black worshippers at an outdoor camp meeting in 1817 marching around an outdoor tabernacle, singing a spiritual chorus and blowing a trumpet, in a reenactment of the march around Jericho by Joshua and the Israelites that is similar to the march that the Singing and Praying Bands continue to do today.[22] If we look at these historical references with minds informed by the bands of today, we can project the current tradition to have been already thriving two hundred years ago, in the early years of the nineteenth century.

This nascent African American expressive culture articulated new belief systems that were forming among Africans in this area, also to a certain extent in the context of Protestant evangelism. Africans in America developed a variant of this branch of Protestantism that expressed protonationalist African American identity.[23] According to this theology of resistance, African American Christians began to associate their experience in America with that of the Israelites in Egypt, and the person of Jesus took on some of the qualities of Moses, who would not fail to liberate the enslaved.[24] It was to some extent in the religious meetings of the upper South and in the language of this distinctive African American perspective that Gabriel Prosser and Nat Turner situated their rebellions in Virginia.[25]

Much of this theology of liberation is articulated in the lyrics of spirituals from the nineteenth century.[26] Unnamed folk authors, composers, and thinkers created a belief system in which, for example, Moses told Pharaoh, in strikingly contemporary terms, to "let my people go." Many have come to associate this song with Harriet Tubman and her remarkable efforts to bring the enslaved people out of bondage in Maryland.[27] In another lyric, talk of being "bound for Canaan land" might refer to escape from slavery into the North, as Frederick Douglass described the disguised intent of singers in his community, also in eastern Maryland.[28] Still other song texts from this area referred to Joshua and the Israelites shouting down the walls of Jericho, celebrating the hope of a revolutionary victory over the current rulers of the land.[29]

The enslaved Africans who became involved in this movement understood this revolutionary victory to be implicit in their recognition of the divinity of a loving, suffering, and very human savior, who died betrayed and brokenhearted, who was resurrected, and who would similarly redeem the downtrodden and brokenhearted who identified with him. In a religious system that blended European and African cultural traits, many enslaved Africans metaphorically died, to be reborn as African Americans, for whom the church then became the bedrock of the community. A significant portion of this early culture building took place in the Atlantic coast areas of the upper South.

Finally, the tidewater areas of the upper Chesapeake and Delaware bays, where the antecedents to Singing and Praying Bands seem to have been almost ubiquitous, also gave rise to some of the great early African American leaders. Richard Allen spent his early years in Philadelphia and in Kent County, Delaware. Harriet Tubman grew up in a small hamlet in Dorchester County, Maryland, just south of the city of Cambridge. Frederick Douglass was born and grew up near Easton, in Talbot County, Maryland, subsequently moving to Baltimore. Later black leaders, such as Charles Albert Tindley—who was born and raised in Worcester County, Maryland—also hailed from this area. Descendants of collateral branches of the Tubman and Ross (Harriet's maiden name) families and members of the Tindley family have been active in the bands until very recently.

Because of their multifaceted importance in the development of early African American culture, the upper South and the mid-Atlantic region can be considered among the hearth areas in which African American culture took shape. Significantly, evidence also suggests that in much of the area surrounding Delaware Bay and the upper Chesapeake, the groups that eventually formed the Singing and Praying Bands were the predominant grassroots, African American, folk religious institutions. As such, they were a part of the cultural legacy that anonymous slaves may have carried with them in their forced journey south.

There is no direct documentation connecting the bands to later traditions in the Deep South and the Gulf Coast. Yet I maintain that the Singing and Praying Bands—and the African-based spirituality growing out of patterns of reciprocity and mutual aid that they represent—were central to the formation of grassroots African American religion in this one hearth area. They can be viewed, therefore, as a prominent folk religious tradition in a region central to the development of African American foundational culture. The bands of today form one of the oldest traditions of African American music still extant. Perhaps the early predecessors of the Singing and Praying Bands can also be viewed as prototypes of African American folk religious cultures that developed elsewhere in the country.

The camp meetings and the Singing and Praying Bands have not yet been consigned to the annals of history. In tidewater Maryland and Delaware a good number of brave souls and resolute churches continue, against overwhelming odds, to keep the tradition alive. All of these individuals, and the churches to which they belong, continue to be Methodist—not Baptist, not Pentecostal, not Holiness, or any other denomination. At its height, this particular camp-meeting tradition seems to have included all of the tidewater areas—the Chesapeake area of Maryland, the Eastern Shore of Virginia, most of Delaware, parts of southern New Jersey, and southeastern Pennsylvania—surrounding Philadelphia and Baltimore. These latter cities were two of the early centers of American Methodism in general, both the Methodist Episcopal and the African Methodist Episcopal churches in particular.[30] Today, the bands remain only in a few areas of the Eastern Shore of Maryland and southern Delaware; in Anne Arundel County, Maryland; and in the city of Baltimore.

The Singing and Praying Bands are not musical groups as the word "band" would seem to imply to outsiders. The term "prayer band" derives from John Wesley's use of the term "band society" to describe the organization of the prayer meetings held by each congregation of his Methodist movement.[31] By the nineteenth century, the term "prayer band" had become common in Methodism in the United States. In the twentieth century, many black churches in America continued to maintain prayer bands. In tidewater Maryland and Delaware, where the bands persist to this day, the term "Singing and Praying Band" has come to refer specifically to those groups that grew out of the local Methodist prayer meetings, in the various Methodist denominations, in churches throughout the region.

The old-time prayer meetings were fascinating services in their own right. The "faithful few" in each Methodist congregation attended these prayer meetings on Sunday evenings and weeknights throughout the year, year in and year out. In the past, many churches did not have large gospel choirs, with the elaborate musical arrangements, fancy robes, and well-trained directors that are common today. Instead, after a preacher preached a sermon, many in the congregation would remain in service, singing hymn after hymn, praying impassioned prayers, building up the spirit. This would be the prayer meeting.

From year to year and from place to place, a prayer meeting unfolded in a recognizable pattern. The people at the prayer meeting raised a hymn and "labored" with that hymn; they "tarried" in the meeting until their singing became lively and the Spirit enlivened their words. That Spirit entered into the clapping of their hands and the patting of their feet, into the very movements of their bodies. It changed their emotions and penetrated their souls. As the Spirit "ran from heart to heart and from breast to breast," the people would begin to shout and whoop as a reaction to this renewed blessing, as Mary Allen, Gertrude Stanley, and Rev. Edward Johnson describe in later chapters of this book.

These meetings did not simply cater to the faithful. Leaders from the community would place an old bench that they called a mourners' bench in the front of the sanctuary, between the first row of the pews and the altar. Those seeking to be saved would come forward and kneel beside this bench to pray. Members of the prayer meeting would stand around the kneeling mourners, singing around them and praying over them until they "came through," until, that is, they felt the Spirit for the first time. The mourners would thus be converted.

There were some variations in this pattern. In a few churches, members of the group would sit in the pews when they began to sing; in other churches, they would stand in front from the beginning, a straight line of men on one side of the mourners' bench facing a line of women on the other side. In some churches, they would begin the prayer meeting by "lining out" popular, multiversed Methodist hymns. That is, a leader would chant a line of the hymn, and the group would sing it in response. In other churches, a congregation might sing a hymn straight through from memory, without a leader. In still other churches, however, those in the congregation might start out standing in a circle in the front of the sanctuary, sing a spiritual song that a community member or his or her parents or grandparents had created, and continue the meeting by singing other, increasingly lively spirituals.

In all churches, however, these meetings always came to an end with a bang and not a whimper. Whether the participants began the meeting sitting down in the pews or standing up in front, at the end of the service they would all come forward to the altar area, push the pews back, form a circle, and sing an exuberant spiritual chorus, clapping their hands all the while, shouting, and getting happy. This animated singing often culminated in a counterclockwise march around the mourners' bench and a march around the inside of the sanctuary.

In black churches, this type of spirited song service, performed in a circle and sung with the whole body, is usually referred to as a "shout." The shout and the circle are important. In the coastal areas of the Deep South, participants called this ritual more specifically a ring shout.[32] Scholars of African American history and religion have adopted the term for this kind of service from them. In their influential book *Folksong USA*, the folklorists John and Alan Lomax offered a definition of the ring shout after witnessing it in the American South. The ring shout, they maintained, is not just sung but is danced with the whole body; the dancers move counterclockwise around in a circle; the singing maintains a leader-chorus form that emphasizes rhythm rather than melody; and finally, the song is often repeated over a long period of time, escalating in intensity of effort and emotional fervor.[33] Many scholars consider the ring shout to be the earliest form of African American music to survive in North America.

The ring shout is a form of worship that is clearly of West African origin. It preceded evangelical Christianity among the enslaved, becoming Christianized only during the Great Awakening in the early nineteenth century. Before churches were built in their towns, members of slave communities held these Christianized ring shouts in secret places in the forests or fields surrounding a particular settlement. In chapter 5 of this book, Rev. Edward Johnson describes hearing about this from older members of his family.[34] Although African Americans in the Chesapeake area did not use the term "ring shout," these new Christians practiced similar African-derived rituals and brought their "shouts" into their churches.

There are both similarities and differences between the shout traditions that developed in the mid-Atlantic region and the better-known shout tradition that evolved in the coastal Southeast. Both traditions share the basic structures of the ring shout that John and Alan Lomax described, and both seem to be equally historic. Yet scholars know more about the ring shouts of coastal South Carolina and Georgia than they know of those of the mid-Atlantic region. Systematic national attention given to the shouts from the Southeast can be dated to a period when the Civil War was at its height. During that time, Union troops took control of several islands off the coast of South Carolina before the fall of the Confederacy. While the war still raged elsewhere, a number of abolitionists, missionaries, and educators from the North came to the Sea Islands to prepare the freedmen for self-reliance, in what came to be something of a trial run at Reconstruction.[35] Some of these newcomers attended ring shouts during these years, writing articles about them in popular magazines of the time.[36] After the war, several of those who spent time on the Sea Islands published the book *Slave Songs of the United States,* for which some of the fieldwork had been done in the coastal Southeast. Along with song notations, the authors of this book included a description of a ring shout, adding that "in the form here described, the 'shout' is probably confined to South Carolina and the States south of it."[37] Perhaps from that time onward, historians have associated the ring shout with the tidewater areas of the coastal Southeast. Subsequent generations of writers and folklorists flocked to this area, also writing about the ring shouts there.[38]

Unlike reports from the coastal Southeast, the more sporadic eyewitness observations of ring shouts in the mid-Atlantic region were not absorbed into the general literature on African American music, religion, or folklore. Remarkable descriptions of shouts and camp meetings by writers such as Rev. Robert Todd had little impact on scholars of black history. When scholars did cite eyewitness accounts of ring shouts in the mid-Atlantic region by John Fanning Watson or John Dixon Long, they did not note the distinct pattern that these reports reveal, which was different from the pattern of shouts in the Southeast.

Despite the basic similarities of ring shouts that the Lomaxes noted, the shout in the coastal Southeast and the shout in the mid-Atlantic area seemed to have evolved in different directions. While there were many local variations in each tradition, primary sources describing the ring shouts in South Carolina and Georgia often report that the shouters moved in a counterclockwise circle, while a small group of singers off to the side provided accompaniment. One of that supporting group might lead the singing, while another might keep a master beat by pounding the floor with a stick; still others created complex cross-rhythms through clapping.[39] Although songs comprised of simple choruses and rhyming verses are well represented in the literature of African American sacred music of that time and place, shout songs of the region frequently consisted of one line offered by the leader, followed by the burden or chorus, sung by a group.

In the mid-Atlantic region, things were different. Primary references to the shout in this area make almost no mention of the counterclockwise march, or of a band of singers off to the side of the shout group. Instead, many nineteenth-century observers comment that the shout was accompanied by a chorus of several lines repeated over and over, with rhyming verses sometimes added.[40] The leader of the ring shout was found not off to the side, but in the middle of the ring.[41] As often as observers of the ring shout of the Southeast remark upon the counterclockwise march, observers in the mid-Atlantic region note that shouters expressed their religious fervor by leaping, jumping, and springing off the ground, maneuvers not mentioned as frequently further south.[42]

It is perhaps arguable that the ring shouts of the Southeast, with their complex cross-rhythms, subtle dance maneuvers, and antiphonal songs, are closer to West African religious dances than are the mid-Atlantic shouts. Yet when we survey the earliest primary sources on ring shouts in both areas, it seems clear that it is impossible to think of the ring shout as having a single original form—an "ur-form"—from which all of the local traditions developed. Most likely, the shouts of these two hearth areas developed simultaneously and somewhat independently.

While there are differences in the traditions, one similarity is striking. All eyewitness observers of ring shouts refer to their taking place *after* a formal prayer meeting or preaching service had been completed. While this pattern may speak of the efforts of officials of the institutional church to marginalize the shout, it also seems to indicate that the shout was an expression of and culmination of the joy of communion that had been built up during the prior service. Lyrics of shout songs tend to express this joy. Thus lyrics celebrating Gabriel's blowing of a trumpet to signal the end of the current unjust epoch, or memorializing the survival of John, the author of Revelation, on the island of Patmos—or any lyrics in which the probability of future salvation is brought into the present and celebrated through song and worship—are found in both traditions.[43]

A final point of comparison between the ring shout of the mid-Atlantic area and that of the coastal Southeast should be made. While in both traditions, the shout took place after a religious service, its fate seems to have been different in the two areas. In the Deep South, the fervor represented by the ring shout may have been incorporated into the mainstream of Afro-Baptist worship, only to have the classic form of the ring shout itself largely disappear. The highly organized Methodist denominations that dominated African American religious life in the mid-Atlantic region, however, had little use for an ancient form of worship that they did not control. Yet the shout's practitioners were unwilling to give it up entirely. Consequently they found a place for it on the margins of the religious organization of the church. The prayer meetings were not as closely supervised by church officials as were many other church activities; it was in these prayer meetings, therefore, that these new believers felt most free to worship as they always had. It must have seemed quite natural that the shout be appended to the end of these unsupervised events, in a manner that the rare outside observer might interpret as an afterthought.

The people who attended the prayer meetings also organized the camp meetings. Like prayer meetings, the camp meetings were not part of the official practice of the institutional church. That is, the institutional church allowed camp meetings because parishioners wanted them, but the denomination did not require its members to have them, nor did it make them part of official church discipline.[44] At each camp meeting, prayer-meeting groups from the many churches in any one region converged to support each other's large, yearly events. Together, they would crowd into each camp meeting, creating the spectacles that so many people today remember fondly, as described later in this book.

Ensconced within the Methodist churches, the practitioners of this folk tradition of religion came to realize that their practice had become an institution in its own right. They began to refer to their services not just as prayer meetings, but as gatherings of the "Singing and Praying Bands." As institutions, they developed their own leaders, called band captains, which Alfred Green explains in chapter 1. Each band wore distinctive uniforms and maintained an impressive yearly round of services that included prayer meetings, band days at their home churches, and New Year's Eve Watch Night services, as Susanna Watkins explains in chapter 7, and distinct funeral services for deceased members, as Rev. Johnson makes clear in chapter 5. Most especially, each band held camp meetings at their home churches.

The African American camp meetings in this area differed from the frontier camp meetings that have become so well known in American history. Usually they were not held at retreats in the woods. Instead they were most frequently held right in the sponsoring churches' sanctuaries and fellowship halls, with the purpose of raising money for the home church. These camp meetings may have gone on for ten full days or more, and the people who attended them may have left their fields or their jobs in the cities, brought food from home, erected tents, and stayed on the church grounds for the duration. Yet this is not what made these events memorable.

In Maryland and Delaware, the camp meetings are remembered primarily as showcases for the many Singing and Praying Bands that attended them. Because of the great number of bands that came to each camp meeting, a formal system of fellowshipping developed among the different bands that attended each other's meeting. That is, any band that attended another church's camp meeting could expect that the band from that church would reciprocate, as many band members explain in their testimonies in this book. In this way, each camp meeting was guaranteed a large turnout of bands from within this network.

The organizers of the camp meetings within this network developed a specific etiquette to give every band an opportunity to perform. They gave each band a particular day and a particular time to sing. These allotted times became traditional. Year after year, members of each band knew exactly when their turn would come. Many participating bands developed a sense of competition with the others, and each band practiced in advance to ensure its preparedness. Although band uniforms tended to be similar among all the bands—a simple cotton jacket for the men, a black or white dress for the women, augmented by a white apron—specific bands adopted variations on this pattern. The distinctive uniforms enabled those who attended a camp meeting to identify the home church of each band.

The system of fellowshipping and the playful competition among the bands turned each camp meeting into something of a spectacle. Camp meetings became regional festivals of folk religion. The network of camp meetings can be considered, therefore, to be a loosely organized folk religion that celebrates its African roots while surviving under the umbrella of the various Methodist churches.[45] Because the Singing and Praying Bands continue one of the oldest traditions of African American religious song and worship, one that forms a bridge between African identities and African American identity, the bands of today are of great significance to African American culture.

To this day, from March until December, each Singing and Praying Band still travels as an organized group from one band day or camp meeting to the next, Sunday after Sunday. In the 1950s, however, the Singing and Praying Band tradition started to decline. Older members from the heyday of the camp meetings began to die out. Younger church members preferred to sing in newer gospel quartets and choirs. The liberalization of society in general tended to affect adversely those staunchly conservative religious organizations that, like the bands, survived within the various mainstream Protestant denominations. Bands from churches in Philadelphia, Wilmington, Washington, D.C., and the Eastern Shore of Virginia began to drop out of the network. Gradually, each band lost so many members that no single band could hold a spirited service on its own.

Responding to this decline, all the remaining bands decided to consolidate into two performing ensembles. The bands from churches in Delaware and the Eastern Shore of the Chesapeake perform together, and the bands from the Western Shore of the Chesapeake perform together. Only a few churches in the band network still sponsor the full, ten-day camp meetings of old. Several churches continue to have camp meeting on two successive Sundays, a vestige of the era when most camp meetings included two full weekends. Frequently, however, the extended hubbub characteristic of camp meetings has been concentrated in a single Sunday-evening service.

These shortened meetings often proceed according to an established plan. When all bands are attending a camp meeting at a church on the Western Shore, the Eastern Shore bands hold a prayer meeting first. Often they sing after an early afternoon preaching service so that they can get on the road sooner and get home at a reasonable hour. The Western Shore bands then sing after an evening preaching service. The reverse holds true when the host church is on the Eastern Shore. When a camp meeting still spans two Sundays in a row, one group will perform the first Sunday, and the other on the closing Sunday. Although individual bands no longer hold services on their own, each band from each church maintains its own identity and its own leadership, even when having service in combination with bands from other churches. In this way, the grand camp meetings of the past and the Singing and Praying Bands have continued, albeit in a briefer form.

The sequence of events at today's truncated camp meetings remains constant from church to church. A class meeting—what is sometimes called an experience service—features a plethora of individual testimonies and begins an afternoon or evening meeting. Next, a popular guest minister with a reputation for moving a church presides over the preaching service. Usually, this minister will bring a gospel choir from his charge with him to sing. The minister of the home church monitors the event from the sidelines. After the offering has been taken, and after the visiting minister has surrendered control over the proceedings to the host captain, band members scattered throughout the sanctuary rise from their seats in the pews and move forward to begin the band service in the cross aisle of the church, between the front pew and the altar. In the old days, some worshippers might begin the hymn-singing part of the prayer meeting while seated in the pews. But since the formation of the bands, the whole group stands in the front of the church from the beginning: the prayer meeting and the ring shout have been combined into one indivisible service. Several of the men set up an old mourners' bench or a line of folding chairs in front of the altar. One or two rows of men stand behind the bench, on the altar side, facing the congregation, while the women of the bands similarly form two rows facing the men, the bench or chairs separating the two sexes. In times past, "mourners" would come and kneel at the mourners' bench and the bands would sing and pray over them. Today, mourners seldom come forward. Churches only rarely have a mourners' bench on hand, and the bands have reluctantly accepted the row of metal folding chairs that they now must use to separate the men from the women.

The Singing and Praying Band service unfolds with startling regularity. It begins with a hymn and a prayer, follows with a second hymn and prayer in the same pattern, and concludes with an ebulliently sung spiritual. During the concluding spiritual, the group begins to march, first counterclockwise around the row of folding chairs, then around the perimeter of the sanctuary, and finally out of the church and onto the church grounds.

But at the beginning of the service, the host captain calls on one of the visiting captains to raise the first hymn. This captain can lead the hymn himself, or he can designate a member of his band to lead. If a man is chosen to lead, he will move to the center of the row of men with the sisters' captain directly opposite him. If a woman is chosen to lead the hymn, she stands in the center of the row of women facing the men's captain of her band. Together, this central couple raises the first hymn. Usually, the leader will choose a hymn with a penitential theme to begin the service. Hymns that emphasize the immediacy of death and the inevitability of judgment—hymns such as "And Am I Born to Die?" by Charles Wesley (1707–88), or "That Awful Day Must Surely Come," by Isaac Watts (1674–1748)—tend to predominate. The leader "gives out" the hymn, as the band members say, line by line. Hymns raised in this manner are referred to, plainly, as a "give-out hymns." The band tradition usually offers a leader several tunes in which he or she can sing each hymn text.

The leader of the first hymn starts the service slowly and tentatively. He begins a give-out hymn by singing the first line of the hymn through, slowly and at a low pitch, so that those standing near the center can catch both the text and the tune. The singing ensemble sings each line two times. By the end of the second repetition of the first line, everyone in the group will have recognized the hymn and begun to sing along. The leader then gives out the second line of the text in a chant, the melodic contour of which resembles the tune in which he or she has decided to raise the hymn. At first, as the group struggles to catch on, the singing is wooden. It takes time and effort to raise a hymn, as Mary Allen and Samuel Jerry Colbert attest in subsequent chapters.

The term "raising a hymn" accurately summarizes this process in which the singing only gradually becomes lively. Line by line, beginning in slower-than-slow tempos, ornamenting each note of the basic melody with multiple grace notes, the hymn leader leads the group through a hymn; line by line, the group finds itself inexorably raising the pitch of the hymn and increasing its tempo, clapping their hands and patting their feet on the wooden floor to accent the melody with percussive punctuation. With each escalation of pitch and tempo, with each louder clap, each individual intensifies his or her physical involvement in the religious experience. As the singers become more sure of themselves, they pat their right feet on the floor while swaying to the right; they follow this motion by clapping their hands. Then they sway to the left, patting their left feet on the floor; they then clap again. The entire singing group keeps up this four-beat pattern throughout the hymn. Sometimes the church itself becomes like a drum, as the sound of the stamping feet establishes a master beat that reverberates throughout the building.

But this is just the beginning. When the hymn leader has completely given out the text, he may add an additional verse to the text, a verse drawn from another hymn. Favorite closing verses float freely from hymn to hymn. Band members like to extend their singing by repeating the last line of this favorite verse over and over as a chanted meditation. Thus, the band leader may add this verse—or one like it—to any number of hymns: "Oh weeping friend, don't weep for me while standing around my bed; / I know the way to Galilee; thank God I have no dread." The group often sings the last line of this verse over and over, changing the melody somewhat, restricting its melodic range and accentuating the rhythmic features of the singing. When the whole group sings in unison, individuals add their own embellishments, giving the singing a dynamic quality in which each voice stands out because each person sings slightly differently from the others. Band members refer to the achievement of this effortless unison as getting "on one accord," like the original disciples on the day of Pentecost (Acts 2:1–3). During this excited chant, individual embellishments on the basic melody grow into "whoops," and then the whooping becomes shouting. Those who get happy wave their hands and jump and cry out, "Oh yes!" or "Look out!" or "Come on!" The women and men at the ends of the rows turn toward the center; for the first time in the service, what began as straight lines of men and women begins to resemble a circle of singers.

In theory, the bands could sing this last line over and over all night. Yet invariably, the leader who raised the hymn, his task done, steps aside to let the captain from another church move to the center. This captain calls down the hymn, gradually letting the shout subside. He then calls on one of the supplicants, a member of his band, to pray the first prayer.

A long and impassioned prayer follows. When individuals join a band, they require of themselves a preparedness to sing and pray as if today itself might be the Day of Judgment. The intensity of expression is not limited to the prayer-giver but is found among the respondents as well, who loudly affirm each statement the prayer-giver makes. The band members refer to this responding as "helping" the prayer-giver. They cite a biblical passage to support their effort to be prepared: "Watch therefore: for ye know not what hour your Lord doth come" (Matthew 24:42). Each band member comes prepared to help the others; this assurance of support from all others present encourages each prayer-giver to pray as if it is his or her last prayer.

A prayer-giver invariably uses a conservative prayer structure and a mostly formulaic vocabulary to express the feelings that are in her heart at the moment of prayer. Since the institution of the bands is an old one, the prayers of the band members redound with a rich body of images, built up through the years, and a somewhat old-fashioned vocabulary. The praying person improvises her prayer using familiar phrases drawn from favorite hymn texts, spirituals and gospel songs, proverbial expressions, and established prayer motifs that make up this oral tradition. Although the supplicant does not compose the prayer in advance, she usually begins the prayer with a recitation of a favorite hymn text, to establish both the tone of the prayer and its cadence. She then offers praise and thanksgiving to God for past blessings and expresses the continuing need for God's intercession in our lives.

At the beginning of the prayer, the others in the prayer meeting will nod and affirm the words of the praying person, reassuring the supplicant by saying, "It's okay, Ruth," or "Take your time, Nettie," or by repeating—as is the fashion in this overlapping call-and-response style of performance—the supplicant's words after her. If the prayer-giver says, "You are the lily," the others help complete the phrase, saying, "of the valley." When the prayer-giver goes on to say, "You are the bright," the others will pitch in, saying, "and the morning star." Both the prayer-giver and the listeners may complete these statements of praise, saying together, "You are the root and the branch of David." After all, the words, while always appropriate to the moment, also belong to the traditional vocabulary of prayer, and as such they are recognizable to the listeners.

Following the prayer of thanksgiving, the praying person then asks of God a series of petitions. This series of petitions begins with a highly stressed and poetically expressed invocation for God to send his Holy Spirit to bless the congregation right then and there. A prayer-giver has many traditional invocations from which to choose. One frequently heard invocation goes like this:

We are praying that you might come this evening, our Father
        over the hills and the mountains,
    bringing free grace in one hand,
    bring pardon in the other,
    and bind up these wounds
        that sin has caused all over the land.[46]

Following the invocation, a prayer-giver might ask God to intercede in our lives of today: "Bless the sick," he might implore, "the poor and the needy, the distressed and the unconcerned." And further:

We are praying this evening, our Father,
    For those that are out of the arc of safety,
        those that are walking up and down the highway of life,
            straying to the right and to the left,
                don't care for God nor man.
We pray this evening
    that you might shake them over the fiery pits of Hell,
        and suffer them not to fall.
    And they that cry out
        are due to be saved.[47]

With each petition, the urgency of the prayer-giver increases; the congregation then meets the praying person's enthusiasm with its own. The fervor escalates until the praying person, perhaps walking up and down the center aisle, perhaps swept off her feet by emotion and propped up by several sisters, may ask God to grant her a future home in heaven, where she can "walk in Jerusalem just like John," and "where the wicked will cease from troubling; our weary souls will be at rest."

Each prayer concludes with a formal "amen" statement. Having begun with a recitation, the praying person moves the body of the prayer from thanksgiving to invocation to petitions, from the past to the present to the future, with the prayer as a whole focused on the invocation. The prayer is complete.

The mood of the prayer meeting tends to shift with the invocation in a prayer that calls on the Holy Spirit to become present among the congregation then and there. That is, like the prayer, the beginning of the meeting is somber, emphasizing human unworthiness in the face of judgment, while the conclusion is joyful. There are good reasons why this shift occurs. When the band members meditate on the penitential words of the opening hymn, or the beginning of the prayer, they become a repentant community, one in which each band member asks for forgiveness from God and from each other. The sincerity of this repentance fuels the escalating fervor of both the singing and praying. Eventually, a spirit of love replaces the spirit of petty jealousy and tension that all too often animates everyday group interaction. The shout breaks out as the group builds enough spiritual power for this spirit of love to become manifest among them. A sense of redemption replaces the feeling of being heavy laden. At some moment, almost everyone present feels the breath of the Holy Spirit hover over the congregation, before it swoops down onto them. During a prayer, some may fall out flat, others might run or laugh. During the shout itself, some people will jump or shout out; always some will shed tears of joy.

The Spirit revives the band members. Its successful invocation can give them a foretaste of heaven. The extraordinary spiritual power of the bands to invoke the Holy Spirit also made them effective agents in the cause of converting mourners, who would be born again as believers. As an instrument helping to effect the symbolic death of a sinner and the salvation of the soul, the shout became crucial also at funerals for band members, the time of the death of the body and the hoped-for resurrection of the soul.[48]

While the praying person composes herself, smoothing her apron, drying the tears, returning to the world of the here and now, the others in the prayer meeting move on to a second hymn. The bands begin this hymn with more certainty, building it on a reestablished sense of community solidarity. Once again, a new hymn leader guides the prayer meeting, line by line, through the hymn using her tune of choice. Again, the members of the ensemble raise the pitch, tempo, and loudness of the singing as they proceed, clapping hands and patting feet all along, throwing themselves with greater abandon into the religious devotion, until the leader calls down the hymn and designates a prayer-giver for a second prayer.

After this prayer, it is time for a final hymn, the shout, and the march. While the band members are still on their knees at the conclusion of the second prayer, another band captain begins a different kind of hymn, one that band members call a "straight hymn." It is with this hymn that the prayer meeting will end. Outsiders might call these straight hymns "spirituals," but members of the band never use that term. They are called straight hymns because they are so simple in both words and tune that everyone in the group can sing them straight through from memory, without the need of a leader to give it out. These songs usually evoke a single, often joyful biblical image. One popular straight hymn recounts some of the words spoken by Jesus, when he arose from the dead (Matt. 28:7):

> Oh Mary, Oh Martha,
> Go and tell my disciples
> To meet me in Galilee.

A simple hymn like this does not take as long to raise as a give-out hymn. The group as a whole sings the chorus through three or four times while on their knees; then they rise to their feet and again sway to the left and to the right, clapping their hands and patting their feet, each worshipper using his or her whole body in the shout. In the band tradition, this movement is not called dancing, but motioning, as Cordonsal Walters explains in chapter 6. As they did earlier with the give-out hymns and prayers, the performing group begins the straight hymn slowly and then builds it up in pitch and tempo and spiritedness. When the members of the group are all singing and swaying together, the leader of the straight hymn adds a narrative couplet at the end of one repetition of the chorus. The rest of the group picks up on this added verse as soon as they recognize the new words, singing along with the leader, like the responses to the words of the prayer-giver, in an overlapping call-and-response pattern, as Mary Allen explains in chapter 2. These rhymed couplets, or verses, usually describe a memorable event from the Bible in a concise form. The verses have been handed down from generation to generation, descending from a time when few could read. The story of doubting Thomas (John 20:24–29), for example, is summarized in one two-line verse: "Christ told Thomas 'I am the man.' / Look at the nail prints in my hand." The leader adds several of these verses to the hymn, before gesturing to another band member to step in and add others. Then, one person after another adds new verses to the repetitious chorus.

The prayer band service ends joyfully, as one would expect from a service that has invoked the Spirit. In practice, this means that the words of the straight hymns and its verses tend to be as ebullient as the words of initial give-out hymns are penitential. The presence of the Holy Spirit has lent renewed vigor to the worshippers and has given them a sense of assurance of salvation. As living witnesses to the Spirit, members of the bands think of themselves as the religious descendants of the prophets, the judges, kings, disciples, and martyrs of the Bible. They feel aligned with the bravery of Moses, with the faith of Job, the trials of Daniel, the visions of John. They express their witness through increasingly spirited singing and shouting and motioning, bowing, waving, jumping, and gesturing. As the men singers and women singers at the ends of the lines on either side of the mourners' bench again begin to turn inward and look toward the hymn leader, the shouting group transforms itself subtly into a shouting circle.

Yet even this intense witness is not sufficient for the band members. The members of the prayer bands want to take their understanding to the world. Having placed themselves in the long tradition of biblical heroes, they continue one of these traditions: they march. They march as the Israelites marched around Jericho, as a conquering army who took this city in the promised land by nonviolently shouting down its walls. Likewise, the bands march out into the world as conquerors intent on shouting down the walls of sin that surround the hearts of the sinners.

The triumphant spirit of this march is difficult to miss. First, the group marches counterclockwise around the mourners' bench, in a maneuver clearly related to the ring shouts of an earlier era, as Cordonsal Walters recounts later in this book. Several band members explain this as something of a role reversal: men and women begin the service standing on opposite sides of the mourners' bench in the same way that, in the Methodist past, they would sit on opposite sides of the sanctuary, in rows of pews separated by the center aisle. This is something Samuel Jerry Colbert recalls in this book. In the circular march around the mourners' bench, the women move to the men's side of the bench, to face the congregation and, for a few moments, to take a leadership role in the band singing. This role reversal is something of a relic of the past, when women were allowed few leadership roles in the church. Today, when women routinely take the lead in many church activities, the counterclockwise march has diminished in importance.

Yet where space to march exists, band members still march. After circling the mourners' bench one or possibly two times, they march excitedly around the inside perimeter of the church building, gesturing, preaching, and prophesying to those few who might have remained seated. If the weather permits, the whole group marches out of the church building and onto the church grounds. Clapping constantly as they sing, the marching group periodically stops on the church grounds, regrouping as a circle of singers, facing inward, into the center of which a succession of new leaders, men or women, may step to add their favorite verses. If the weather is cold or rainy, the band members eschew the march outside and return instead to the front of the church, where they regroup into a circle and sing the straight hymn several times over again, adding more verses. Gradually the singing dies down. The prayer meeting is over.

Things were not so simple in the past. At one time, so many bands showed up on the last day of the large camp meetings that two or three bands might be scheduled to sing and pray after each preaching service. When one band finished singing in church and marched out, another band would be waiting to march into the church, to hold their prayer meeting and to march out, joining other bands that would be singing in separate circles on the campgrounds, as Alfred Green and Rev. Johnson later elucidate. Another testimony service and another preaching service would begin in the sanctuary; three hours later, when these were complete, still more Singing and Praying Bands would take the stage. In this way, several bands would be singing on the campgrounds at all times. With fires of blazing pine stumps lighting up the night, crowds of onlookers, saints and sinners alike, would crowd around each band to witness the spectacle. This grand finale to the camp meeting often went on all night. It must have been an awesome spectacle indeed: Singing and Praying Band members of today lower their voices, their eyes glow, and a look of wonder steals across their faces as they describe the scene. They have witnessed something great, and they know it.

These events were indeed great. In everyday life, members of the communities that gave rise to the bands faced backbreaking work and economic, social, and political oppression. But in those circles of worshippers, facing inward and singing and clapping, band members create for themselves an ideal community. It works like this. During this service, as previously mentioned, the shout breaks out when a redemptive feeling of love suffuses their efforts in song and prayer. The spirit comes as they get on one accord aesthetically and as a community. This accord underlies the transformation from penitence to jubilation. The group accord also transforms the bands into a singing circle, a natural form for a community, a form in which each member faces the others in a position of equality, and each contributes to the shared vision. In short, they enact an idealized community.

Members of the Singing and Praying Bands refer to their building of this spiritual unity as "laboring in the spirit." The ideal of working together as a community, however, was not limited to the bands or to the churches in which the bands thrived. This collaborative labor in religious matters was but a spiritual distillation of a larger cultural pattern of collaborative labor in economic and social affairs.[49] The bands drew their strength from the strengths of the residents of the small hamlets that African Americans set up for themselves in this area after Emancipation. And in these towns people relied primarily on each other to endure hard times.

Residents of those towns developed strong traditions of mutual aid in economic affairs. One family would help other families in planting and in harvesting. Men in small boats on the Chesapeake would help each other tong for oysters; women in the oyster-shucking houses helped each other keep up their spirits by singing and working together in synchronized rhythms, just as the bands keep in rhythm with their clapping and foot patting, as Rev. Edward Johnson reminisces here. Neighboring families helped each other when hog-killing time came and when the slaughtered hog had to be smoked or pickled or canned, as Cordonsal Walters recalls in chapter 6 of this book. Frequently, the communities that developed such patterns of reciprocity were not composed only of neighboring families; in Frankford, Delaware, they *were* family, as Benjamin and George Beckett explain in chapter 8.[50] The ring shout in their area, as perhaps elsewhere, seems to have been maintained by a multigenerational network of kin.[51] People today who remember those times never cease talking about how wonderful the community life was in those days.

But the people of this region were not unique in their reliance on traditions of mutual support. Since antebellum times, free blacks had similarly relied on mutual aid organizations for their survival. In his book *The Philadelphia Negro*, W. E. B. DuBois commented on the early growth of mutual aid organizations among free blacks, noting that "from early times, the precarious economic condition of the free Negro led to many mutual aid organizations. . . . Confined to a few members, all personally known to each other, such societies were successful from the beginning."[52] An important concept was born.

In rural Maryland and Delaware, however, mutual aid was not limited to matters of subsistence. Just as neighbors helped each other in economic matters, so also did they help each other in areas of social concern. Child rearing tended to be the responsibility of a whole town. And one person's sickness or another person's death mobilized everyone to offer solace. Above and beyond even such tender social support, everyone came together to help the others in their religious affairs. Further, just as they helped each other in the church in general, they helped each other in the prayer bands in particular. And each prayer band helped the other prayer bands; that is, each prayer band attended the camp meeting at another prayer band's home church to *help* that church. In return, a visiting band could expect the help of other bands at its church during its camp meeting. The term that the Singing and Praying Bands use for mutual aid in general and for this network of fellowshipping in particular is simply "help"; "we *help* each other," they say.

But the concept of *help* referred to more than the social organization of the Singing and Praying Bands and to more than that of their home communities. In the prayer meetings, helping each other is also a principle of aesthetics, as described earlier. If one person leads a hymn, all the others sing with all their hearts to help that leader. If one prays, the band members respond to her words to help that prayer-giver. If an individual steps into the center of the circle at the end of the prayer band service and introduces a new verse to a straight hymn, the others surrounding him in the circle immediately pick up that verse and sing it right back to him as a response. Susanna Watkins explains this process in her testimony in chapter 7 of this book.

This aesthetic aspect of the mutual aid—or help—can be summed up with the term "call-and-response." In his book *African Art in Motion*, Robert Farris Thompson has referred to such call-and-response as more than an aesthetic style; it is a musical enactment of community. It represents, in his words, "perfected social interaction."[53] In a sense, the aesthetics of the band service, in which traditions of mutual aid are stripped of their utilitarian concerns and distilled to their spiritual essence, are the highest form of expression of these local traditions of economic, social, and spiritual mutual aid. And of equal importance, this type of call-and-response singing, in which the leader's call overlaps musically with the group's response, is of African origin in both social organization and artistic style.[54]

The ring shout—with the leader singing solo in the center and the others responding from their positions in the surrounding circle—is a natural corollary to the overlapping call-and-response style of singing as an enactment of perfected community. Just as this singing style is clearly African in origin, the circular, group shout as a ritual enactment of community also originated in Africa.[55] The religious spirit and ritual form of the bands, then, can be said to derive from West Africa, and it is all about community.

The counterclockwise march can be considered a further extension of this idea of perfection. The march within the circle implies that the traditions of sacred reciprocity on which the religious service is built—the notion of "help" itself—are continuously unfolding and constantly in motion. The system of fellowshipping within the network of band churches, in the past attuned to the agricultural calendar, is only completely articulated over the course of a full year. The march around the circle, during which each member of the group rotates for a moment through the central position of leadership usually occupied by the hymn leader, represents the balance between the roles of women and men, as explained earlier, as well as the yearly round of reciprocity among groups of kin, in-laws, and potential in-laws. This march can arguably be viewed as aligning the patterns of reciprocity within these communities with the cycles of the nature, enacting through this circular motion a society in harmony not only with itself, but also with the creation.[56]

While the Singing and Praying Band members of today are quite articulate about the bands' history over the last one hundred years and about their own traditions of reciprocity, they remember much less about the earlier history of the shout. In this context then, a researcher from outside the community can reconnect the Singing and Praying Band members of today, their churches, and the public at large with the historical record of how this African-derived religious performance adapted and endured in one region of America.

The mists of history have not closed completely around the early days of the Singing and Praying Bands. Using written sources heretofore unknown to band members, we can develop a working idea of how the band service originated in Africa, traveled to North America, intersected with Christianity, and survived within the church. As previously mentioned, historians and musicologists usually refer to African American shouts, in which participants form a circle, facing inward, and use their whole bodies in the performance, as "ring shouts." It is well known that many West African religious dance traditions contain similar circle dances and include a counterclockwise movement around the ring. Most nineteenth- and early twentieth-century observers of the North American ring shout, therefore, simply took it for granted that it was of African origin. In 1863, a magazine called the *Continental Monthly*, for example, published this description of the shout, in which a white southerner explained it to a visiting Englishman:

> "Did you ever see a *shout*, Mr. _____?"
> I responded in the negative, and inquired what it was.
> "Oh, a dance of negro men and women to the accompaniment of their own voices It's of no particular figure and they sing to no particular tune, improvising both at pleasure, and keeping it up for an hour together. I'll defy you to look at it without thinking of Ashantee or Dahomey; it's so suggestive of aboriginal Africa."[57]

Similarly, in the preface to *The Books of the American Negro Spirituals*, James Weldon Johnson stated that the shout "is nothing more or less than the survival of a primitive African dance."[58] He wrote that similar dances had persisted in Haiti, as he had seen himself, in the West Indies in general, and in parts of South America. More than just replicating the form of African dance, the shout retained some of the religious ethos of Africa, as many observers noted. John and Alan Lomax, for example, concluded definitively that "this 'shout pattern' . . . is demonstrably West African in origin."[59]

The ring shout does share a number of qualities with West African religious dances. In these African dances, as in the shout, members of a group of worshippers form a circle, sing and dance, and move about in a counterclockwise direction, while some who have come under the influence of the possession trance move into the center of the circle. In the *The Myth of the Negro Past*, the anthropologist Melville Herskovits described such West African rituals:

> As a rule, possession comes on at some ceremony where a follower of a god is moved by the singing, dancing, and drumming of a group of which he is a member.

. . . The worshipper to be possessed begins by clapping his hands, nodding his head, and patting his feet in time to the rhythm of the drums. . . . Finally he dashes into the center of the cleared space, where he gives way to the call of his god in the most violent movements conceivable—running, rolling, falling, jumping, spinning, climbing, and later "talking in tongues," and prophesying. As time goes on . . . he subsides and joins the dancers, who always move about the dancing circle in a counterclockwise direction.[60]

In North America, and in the upper South and mid-Atlantic region in particular, similar African-derived religious dances have been noted from the seventeenth century onward. Written observations about the religious life of the enslaved Africans are scarce for the seventeenth and eighteenth centuries. The few historical references that do remain, however, point to the survival of religious dances from Africa. The American system of slavery mingled Africans of various backgrounds. Specific religious services of specific peoples were not, in many cases, reproducible in the New World. Nevertheless, written remarks refer to African-like services. For example, in 1665 an Anglican minister named Rev. Morgan Godwin opined that African slaves in York County, Virginia, engaged in "Idolatrous Dances." We can take his disparaging comment as a reference to non-Christian, African religious dances, for he wrote, "Nothing is more barbarous and contrary to Christianity than their *Idolatrous Dances*, and *Revels*; in which they usually spent the *Sunday*. . . . And here, that I may not be thought too rashly to impute Idolatry to their *Dances*; my conjecture is raised upon this ground . . . for that they use their Dances as a *means* to *procure Rain*."[61]

In a similar vein, the aforementioned minister John Fanning Watson, writing about life in early Philadelphia, observed that many could recall how, prior to the American Revolution, "whole squadrons" of enslaved Africans were allowed to sing and dance during religious "jubilees" in Washington Square on the last days of public fairs. In this case, specific customs of particular African peoples seemed to have remained intact, as Watson noted:

> Many can still remember when the slaves were allowed the last days of the fairs for their jubilee, which they employed ("light hearted wretch [*sic*]!") in dancing the whole afternoon in the present Washington Square, then a general burying ground—the blacks joyful above, while the sleeping dead reposed below! In that field could be seen at once more than one thousand of both sexes, divided into numerous little squads, dancing and singing, "each in their own tongue," after the custom of their several nations in Africa.[62]

In this context, the word "jubilee" almost certainly refers to a tradition of religious rejoicing. This quotation suggests that the pattern that placed African rejoicing at the end of extended celebrations did not begin with camp meetings, but continued a preexisting arrangement. The similarity in pattern between this rejoicing and the later camp meetings suggests that these African-derived religious jubilees were linked to the prayer-meeting circles of nineteenth-century Afro-Christianity. Like the previous example of danced African religion in Virginia, Watson's observation indicates there was a transitional ritual between the religions of Africa and the ring shout.

In this vein, it is important to note that in 1695, Maryland passed a law prohibiting meetings of large numbers of slaves. Further, in 1723, the Maryland Assembly asked that colony's courts to appoint constables to suppress "tumultuous meetings of slaves," considering "the evils resulting from the large meetings of negroes on 'Sabbaths and other Holy-days.'"[63] These laws suggest that spirited Sunday meetings of slaves were quite common, although no record remains of the specific goings-on at these events. Yet we can be fairly certain that African-derived religious worship practices, comprised of combined elements of the practices of many West African peoples, flourished in these areas of America three hundred years ago.

The lack of attention given to the religion of the enslaved changed with the advent of Methodism in the United States at the dawn of the nineteenth century. Maryland and Delaware, where the bands exist today, were important areas in the early history of American Methodism. By the last decade of the eighteenth century, for example, there were twice as many black Methodists in Maryland as in any other state.[64] Methodist missionaries in this region began to notice these African-derived, "tumultuous," danced religious services because the slaves brought this form of worship into Christianity. Perhaps the first to write about this Christian religious "dancing" was Rev. William Colbert, an itinerant Methodist minister. On December 6, 1801, he met with black worshippers in a tidewater town called Potato Neck, in Somerset County, Maryland (today's town of Fairmount). In his journal, he wrote cryptically, "I met the blacks, and a wonderful shout we had, Glory to God. The Lord was prais'd *in the song, in the shout and in the dance* [italic added]."[65]

Generalizing from sources such as this, it appears that from the very beginning of evangelizing, many Africans attempted to Christianize the African-derived danced religious services and bring them into the church. But before many slave communities even had churches, they had clandestine meetings in secret outdoor spots. It seems likely that these secret worship circles predated the advent of Christianity among the enslaved in the plantation South. Yet once Christianity came to them, these same worshippers began to reformulate their African-derived practices according to Christian principles. The practice that Rev. Edward Johnson describes later in this book illustrates this trend. When he details how his grandparents drew a circle on the ground and sang around it, he is describing an African practice of marking religious symbols on the ground as part of rituals that mediate between this world and the next.[66] When he describes how they put a box or a chair in the center to represent a church, he is describing a Christianizing of that African practice. This process was part of a more general reformulation of African beliefs, a process that Melville Herskovits articulated in 1941.[67] In the present book, Cordonsal Walters describes a similar reformulation of African customs when he tells how the counterclockwise movement around in a ring during a prayer meeting, a common feature of West

African religious dancing, became identified by black Christians as a reenactment of the Israelites' marching around Jericho.

It is also seems that slaves thought of the shout—with its focus on the community as a whole, and its direct invocation of the spirit—as their most important ritual. From the beginning they attempted to bring this sensibility into Christianity, and it rivaled and paralleled, for a time, the preaching service as the focus of slave Christianity.[68] Rev. Robert Todd, a historian of Methodism in the Delmarva Peninsula, described, for example, an outdoor shout of enslaved Africans that took place concurrently with protracted meetings of white people in a Methodist chapel on the Eastern Shore of Virginia, the southernmost extension of the Delmarva Peninsula. The fact that these services were simultaneous is important. This juxtaposition perhaps indicates that the enslaved thought of their religious services as comparable in importance to those of the whites. Todd writes, "At Garrison's chapel, in the olden times, great crowds of slaves were wont to assemble; and while the white members, on protracted meeting occasions, rallied around the altar within, the sable soldiers of the cross would repair to the open air, build a camp-fire; and, under the starry canopy of the heavens, form a circle for a holy shout."[69]

While African Americans attempted to bring the shout into the church, many church officials tried to keep out both the overtly pre-Christian *content* and the exuberant worship *style* derived from the African past. Many white missionaries, plantation owners, and, later, some black clergymen looked with suspicion on the "tumultuous" African-derived worship of the enslaved. These leaders seemed to be shocked that the new Christians would associate the physical exhilaration that they got from "dancing" with what the clergy thought of as the sublime peace brought by the in-filling of the Holy Spirit. Anything African was deemed savage at worst and less than orthodox at best.

Attempts to bring the ring shout into Christianity, therefore, met with resistance. The shout was excluded from official practice. In his autobiography, *Recollections of Seventy Years*, Bishop Daniel Alexander Payne of the A.M.E. Church recounted an incident from the mid-nineteenth century that seems to have typified the protracted struggle between the shouters and the institutional church throughout the whole century. When he was the pastor of Bethel A.M.E. in Baltimore, he wrote, "I was enabled to correct some bad customs of worship and especially to moderate the singing and praying bands, which then existed in most extravagant form."[70] The "moderating" effort took place against a backdrop of an extended argument with members of his congregation, an argument that sometimes came to blows. Later still, Bishop Payne wrote more stridently that "the time is at hand when the ministry of the A.M.E. Church must drive out this heathenish mode of worship or drive out all the intelligence, refinement, and practical Christians who may be in her bosom."[71]

This conflict between the shout tradition and the organized church could not have been more clearly stated. This tension eventually was resolved, not by stamping out the shout, but by consigning it to a place at the conclusion of official religious services and on the margins of official church life. Yet at the beginning of the nineteenth century, some ministers who encountered shouting during preaching services simply did not know how to deal with it. Some assumed that the continuation of the African style of worship proved that pre-Christian beliefs still held sway among the African American worshippers. Others, such as William Colbert, had enough "charity" to separate the form of the emotional response from the content of the pre-Christian, African-derived worship. In 1804, he described a love-feast he attended on Maryland's Eastern Shore, in the town of Trapp, in Talbot County: "I do not know when I was among such a noisy people. I left them in high spirits and knew not [what] I could compare the house unto while it was shut up [with] them; than a Bee Hive. There was a mighty roar within. I have so much Charity as to believe the Lord was with them."[72]

A new pattern emerged. Other church officials found the emotional response of the new converts to be disruptive and attempted to delay it until after a preaching service was over. They thereby gave the shouting behavior a place *after* but not *in* official church practice. Another episode, recounted by John Fanning Watson, articulates this trend:

> At the *black* Bethel church in Philadelphia, it has been common to check the immoderate noise of the people, when the preacher has been hindered in his discourse. The Rev. R. S____, when stationed in Philadelphia, after preaching through much acclamation, came down to the altar, saying he had some thing special to communicate. He thus hushed them:—after proceeding a little, a rising murmur, began to drown his voice—and he would appease them again and again in this way—"Stop, stop, my honies [*sic*], not now! bye and bye!" then they would bridle in, and so he and they alternately drew in and let out, till he showed the sign of ending, by waving his handkerchief with the word *now!* Then the whole church was in an instant uproar, jumping and shouting, till "they made the welkin ring."[73]

Perhaps by a happy convergence of two distinct trends, the shout came to be situated after all other church-related worship services were over. In the first of those trends, ministers who apparently tolerated the shouting and jumping *required* it to be delayed to the end, as the religious jubilees of the Africans in Philadelphia's Washington Square had been delayed in the eighteenth century. But second, the shout, as a joyful and cathartic service, *belonged* at the end, as the culmination of worship, not at the beginning or in the middle.

However we attempt to reconstruct events of two hundred years ago, we can say for certain that the ring shout came to find a place for itself on the margins of the institutional church. It came to be performed routinely, first, at the end of prayer meetings and, second, at the camp meetings that the prayer-meeting groups themselves organized. Throughout the nineteenth century, then, observers of the African American ring shout in Maryland, Delaware, and southeastern Pennsylvania wrote about seeing it in those contexts: at the conclusion of prayer meetings and especially at the conclusion of camp meetings.

Written observations of prayer meetings in the black churches of the Philadelphia and Baltimore conferences of the Methodist Episcopal and African Methodist Episcopal churches are rare. Nevertheless, a few references do exist. In his book *Pictures of Slavery in Church and State*, the Methodist minister John Dixon Long describes African American prayer meetings during slavery times in Maryland in a way that is similar to the description given by Cordonsal Walters later in this book:

> The prayer-meetings of the more degraded class of slaves are conducted after the following manner: The colored exhorter or leader calls on two or three in succession to pray, filling up the intervals with singing tunes and words composed by themselves. At a given signal of the leader, the men will take off their jackets, hang up their hats, and tie up their heads with handkerchiefs; the women will tighten their turbans; and the company will form a circle around the singer, and jump and bawl to their heart's [*sic*] content, the women always making more noise than the men.[74]

Similarly, at the end of the nineteenth century, W. E. B. DuBois included in *The Philadelphia Negro* a description of a prayer meeting and ring shout in that city. His account should not sound foreign to the Singing and Praying Bands of today. Again, the shout in this citation was delayed until the end of a prayer meeting, which itself was postponed until after the preaching service had been concluded.

> After a discourse by a very illiterate preacher, hymns were sung, having many repetitions of senseless sentiment and exciting cadences. It took about an hour to work up the congregation to a fervor aimed at. When this was reached a remarkable scene presented itself. The whole congregation pressed forward to an open space before the pulpit, and formed a ring. The most excitable of their number entered the ring, and with clapping hands and contortions led the devotions. Those forming the ring joined in the clapping of hands and wild and loud singing, frequently springing into the air, and shouting loudly. As the devotions proceeded, most of the worshipers took off their coats and vests and hung them on pegs on the wall. This continued for hours, until all were completely exhausted, and some had fainted and been stowed away on benches or the pulpit platform.[75]

These sources show that the African-derived ring shout appended itself to prayer meetings. Other nineteenth-century testimonies make it clear that Africans brought the shout to camp meetings. Those who were very religious held prayer meetings and a ring shout after *each* preaching service of the camp; but the shouters also led the grand, cathartic march around the encampment that came to *conclude* each camp meeting as a whole. As early as 1811, a Rev. Joseph Carson noted in his journal—later to be quoted by William W. Bennett in his book *Memorials of Methodism in Virginia*—that white participants at a camp meeting in Winchester, Virginia, would end the last day of the camp with a final grand march around the encampment.[76] Whether this tradition of the grand march began at that exact moment is indeterminable. It is clear, however, that black worshippers quickly included this march in their services, although they interpreted it differently than did white participants. As the Singing and Praying Band members do today, black worshippers from the beginning seemed to see this march as a reenactment of the Israelites' march around Jericho. In 1817, students from Westtown School witnessed such a march around the encampment at a black camp meeting in Chester County, Pennsylvania. One student's account of this event was published in B. J. Leedom's *Westtown under the Old and New Regime by Auld Lang Syne.*

> As we emerged from the underbrush and entered the opening between the tents, a wild refrain greeted our ears from a portion of the congregation who were marching round the camp, pausing at each corner to blow a tin horn in a blast that rung out in anything but melodious accents upon the summer air; the meaning of which we could not understand, and thought perhaps it might be intended to represent Joshua's chosen men marching around the walls of Jericho, blowing the rams' horns and shouting, until the walls fell. It might have been the intention on this occasion to throw down the walls of sin and permit the prophets of the Lord to have a clear sweep. The refrain, as near as we could make it out, was a monotonous continuation of a few lines from a hymn—
> "We're traveling to Immanuel's land,
>   Glory! Halle-lu-jah!"[77]

The student's account provides a historical record of a tradition that has continued into the twentieth and twenty-first centuries, as Alfred Green describes it in the first chapter of the present book.

Not only had the grand march become the "march around Jericho," but the circular shout had become part of it. In 1819, for example, John Fanning Watson wrote of such outdoor camp-meeting circles of singing and clapping worshippers as an example of what he saw as extravagant worship.

> Here ought to be considered too, a most exceptional error, which has the tolerance at least of the rulers of our camp meetings. In the *blacks'* quarter, the coloured people get together, and sing for hours together, short scraps of disjointed affirmations, pledges, or prayers, lengthened out with long repetition *choruses.* These are all sung in the merry chorus-manner of the southern harvest-field, or husking-frolic method, of the slave blacks; and also very greatly like the Indian dances. With every word so sung, they have a sinking of one or other leg of the body alternately; producing an audible sound of the feet at every step, and as manifest as the steps of actual negro dancing in Virginia, &c. If some, in the meantime sit, they strike the sounds alternately on each thigh.[78]

Observations of practices like these were not uncommon. In the mid-Atlantic states, historians of Methodism somewhat routinely referred to the circular shout among African Americans at camp meetings in the nineteenth century. I. L. Kephart, in his *Biography of J. S. Kessler*, described African American circular shouts in Methodistic camp meetings in the Hagerstown area of western Maryland: "The colored people had their tents in the rear of the preachers' stand, and after preaching they would have their prayer-meetings. They mostly had a circle formed around the altar, composed of singers, and as soon as a mourner was converted they would pass the convert out of that circle into another one, near by, formed for the shouters."[79]

Longer descriptions of camp-meeting ring shouts also survive. Writing about camp meetings on the Delmarva Peninsula during slavery times, Rev. Robert Todd left us with perhaps the best nineteenth-century description of the prayer-meeting tradition of African American Methodists in Maryland. Singing and Praying Band members of today would recognize in his description an antecedent of the prayer meetings of their youth. Todd wrote of the penitential, solemnly sung, lined-out hymn; the rising excitement of the prayer; the transformation of the singing from a long penitential hymn at the beginning into a jubilant spiritual at the end; the formation of a circle of singers; the encircling of a new convert; and the culmination of the camp meeting in a grand march around Jericho. All of these elements are still evident among the Singing and Praying Bands, and the hymns then current are still common among the bands. Rev. Todd's description is so detailed that it deserves to be quoted in full, so that, not long after the turn of the new millennium, we can reconstruct the history of the band service of today.

> In front of their tents, and generally in the most open and sunny spot obtainable, was their shouting-ground, or meeting-place; where, after the sermon, they were wont to gather for the great revival effort. This service was usually opened by the formal announcement of some solemn hymn, such as, "And am I born to die?" or "Hark, from the tomb the doleful sound"; which was sung to a melancholy minor, in the slowest time possible, and slurred and tremoloed into all sorts of fantastic shapes, until the author of old "Mear" or "China," had he listened from the other world, would surely have been unable to recognize his own production. When this opening piece had at last dragged to its conclusion, "Brudder Jacob Isr'el Potter," or "Isaier Ishm'el Carter," or some other recognized dignitary, was called on to "lead in de revotions at de throne ob grace."
>
> Beginning in slow and measured sentences, in indistinct monotone, the petitioner was wont to rise by degrees from apparent formalism to warmth; from warmth to earnestness; from earnestness to intense enthusiasm and excitement; when the prayer and the responses struggled with each other for the mastery in the midst of a confused babel of glowing metaphor and red-hot exclamation; and the conflict was finally terminated by the surrender of the tired lungs and wrecked voice of the leader, to the overpowering noise of superior numbers. The "amen" said, one of the younger and more active "brethering" would spring to the lead in the song-service; and the transition from E flat to C marked the beginning of the jubilant era of "de meetin'." As the leader struck the first notes of the song, peculiar motions, confined to no particular portion or member of the body, indicated the time in which the piece was to be rendered; and significant glances in the direction of the chief "men-singers and women-singers" brought them, one-by-one, into position for effective action, in hollow circle facing inward. The space thus inclosed was devoted to penitents; and there, kneeling on the bare ground—ofttimes prostrate in the dust—many a wounded spirit, from the double bondage, human and satanic, found the liberty of Christ and the "balm in Gilead." . . .

Under the inspiration of sentiments like these, what wonder if ebony faces shone with somewhat of the supernatural fire that illumined Moses' countenance! What wonder if the suddenly unfettered spirit signalled the glad occasion by "walking, and leaping, and praising the Lord!"

Usually the tide of enthusiasm, on the colored side of the encampment, arose and intensified as the days and nights rolled by; and reached the climactic point on the last night of the meeting. By general consent, it was understood that, as to the colored people, the rules requiring quiet after a certain hour, were, on this last night, to be suspended; and great billows of sound from the tornado of praise and singing rolled over the encampment, and was echoed back from hill and wood for miles away, until morrow's dawning. To those in the tents, this hour was usually signalled by the sound of hammer and axe, knocking down the plank partition walls separating the white and colored precincts; and in a few moments, the grand "march 'round de 'campment" was inaugurated, and accompanied with leaping, shuffling, and dancing, after the order of David before the ark when his wife thought he was crazy; accompanied by a song appropriate to the exciting occasion. Some of my readers will recognize the following couplets:

"We's a marchin' away to Cana-ann's land;
I hears de music ob de angel band.
Chorus— "O come an' jine de army;
    An' we'll keep de ark a movin';
    As we goes shoutin' home!
"Come, childering, storm ole Jericho's walls;
Yes, blow an' shout, an' down dey falls!"[80]

Todd was not alone in witnessing African American prayer meeting services at camp meetings. Others also mentioned the singing tradition at African American camp meetings in their memoirs. Writing about his period of ministry in southern Delaware in his memoir, *Fifty Years in the Gospel Ministry, from 1864–1914*, the A.M.E. minister Rev. T. G. Steward commented more cryptically about the camp meeting "after-singing" that he witnessed there, in the late nineteenth century.

The colored people wandered from place to place to attend camp meetings, usually going by stage loads, at a dollar each, in some poor white man's team. These meetings usually ran from Saturday night through Sunday night and were principally occasions for weird singing with the accompaniment of hand clapping. The preaching was of minor importance . . . but the "after-singing" was the feature. I remember one dark Sunday night when the rain was falling rapidly and the crude tents and shacks were flooded, and bedraggled men and women who were practically without shelter made the dismal woods ring with the monotonous song: "Oh, I'd rather be at home, Oh, my Lord." . . . It spoke a philosophy which was doing its best with a bad reputation.[81]

In the present book, Ben and George Beckett also describe this singing.

Finally, the one other long nineteenth-century reference to the Singing and Praying Bands comes from the vitriolic pen of the same Bishop Payne mentioned earlier. Bishop Payne's scorn for the African-derived sensibility of the bands is evident in the following story. He calls this African-derived sensibility "heathenish" and refers to the shout as a "Voudoo Dance." Yet, his writing about the camp meeting illustrates the success of the prayer-meeting groups in taking over the larger camp-meeting tradition, turning these meetings into regional festivals that showcased the incredible survival of their own tradition. Bishop Payne's observation of the bands' successes at the camp meetings unites his testimony with that of Rev. Steward. Both men maintained that the preaching was of little importance but the "after-singing" was the focus of attention. Like Alfred Green, who describes in this book a number of bands singing outdoors at the same time on the final day of his church's camp meeting, Bishop Payne writes that a band leader told him, "At camp-meeting, there must be a ring here, a ring there, and a ring over yonder, or sinners won't get converted." Much as the bands of today still think of themselves as the foundation of the church, the leader told Bishop Payne that the shout remained "the essence of religion."

I have mentioned the "Praying and Singing Bands" elsewhere. The strange delusion that many ignorant but well-meaning people labor under leads me to speak particularly of them. About this time I attended a "bush meeting," where I went to please the pastor whose circuit I was visiting. After the sermon they formed a ring, and with coats off sung, clapped their hands and stamped their feet in a most ridiculous and heathenish way. I requested the pastor to go and stop their dancing. At his request they stopped their dancing and clapping of hands, but remained singing and rocking their bodies to and fro. This they did for about fifteen minutes. I then went, and taking their leader by the arm requested him to desist and to sit down and sing in a rational manner. I told him also that it was a heathenish way to worship and disgraceful to themselves, the race, and the Christian name. In that instance they broke up their ring; but would not sit down, and walked sullenly away. After the sermon in the afternoon, having another opportunity of speaking alone to this young leader of the singing and clapping ring, he said: "Sinners won't get converted unless there is a ring." Said I: "You might sing till you fell down dead, and you would fail to convert a single sinner, because nothing but the Spirit of God and the word of God can convert sinners." He replied: "The Spirit of God works upon people in different ways. At camp meeting there must be a ring here, a ring there, a ring over yonder, or sinners will not get converted." This was his idea, and it is also that of many others. These "Bands" I have had to encounter in many places, and, as I have stated in regard to my early labors in Baltimore, I have been strongly censured because of my efforts to change the mode of worship or modify the extravagances indulged in by the people. In some cases all that I could do was to teach and preach the right, fit, and proper way of serving God. To the most thoughtful and intelligent I usually succeeded in making the "Band" disgusting; but by the ignorant masses, as in the case mentioned, it was regarded as the essence of religion. So much so was this the case that, like this man, they believed no conversion could occur without their agency, nor outside of their own ring could any be a genuine one. Among some of the songs of these "Rings," or "Fist and Heel worshippers," as they have been called, I find a note of two in my journal, which were used in the instance mentioned. As will be seen, they consisted chiefly of what are known as "corn-field ditties":

"Ashes to ashes, dust to dust
If God won't have us, the devil must."
"I was way over there where the coffin fell
I heard that sinner as he screamed in hell."

To indulge in such songs from eight to ten and half-past ten at night was the chief employment of these "Bands." Prayer was only a secondary thing, and this was rude and extravagant to the last degree. The man who had the most powerful pair of lungs was the one who made the best prayer, and he could be heard a square off. He who could sing loudest and longest led the "Band," having his loins girded and a handkerchief in hand with which he kept time, while his feet resounded on the floor like the drumsticks of a bass drum. In some places it was the custom to begin these dances after every night service and keep it up till midnight, sometimes singing and dancing alternately—a short prayer and a long dance. Some one has even called it the "Voudoo Dance." I have remonstrated with a number of pastors for permitting these practices, which vary somewhat in different localities, but have been invariably met with the response that he could not succeed in restraining them, and an attempt to compel them to cease would simply drive them away from our Church.[82]

Bishop Payne misinterpreted the ardent Christianity of the Singing and Praying Bands that he witnessed. There is little doubt that early in the long encounter between African-derived religion in the American South and evangelical Christianity, the practitioners of the clandestine, "danced" worship of Africa became only nominally Christian, as Payne seems to have thought. In the struggle to convert enslaved Africans from their pre-Christian beliefs to a Christian belief system, missionaries and others also attempted to quash the African worship *style*. On the one hand, both white and black elites seemed to believe that the poor and relatively uneducated freedmen needed to be lifted out of the degradation of slavery and out of what the elites thought of as the savagery of Africa. On the other hand, the members of the Singing and Praying Bands, representing a folk tradition, remained steadfast in their practice in which the human body in worship—with the clapping of hands, motioning of the body, patting of feet, the jumping up and down, and the marching—can be considered "an icon of God," with the human heart as his altar, as Albert Raboteau writes in his book *A Fire in the Bones*.[83] This struggle between many of the elites and some of the grassroots faithful resulted in a hundred years of tension between the denominational church and the folk religion that thrived in the area, even though some of the grassroots faithful rejected the ring shout and a number of ministers seemed to accept it.[84] Ironically, by the time Bishop Payne watched the bands with disdain at a camp meeting in 1878, he was not witnessing a heathenish ritual as he supposed; he was witnessing an Afro-centric form of perfectly orthodox Christianity. The process of Christianizing the ring shout had been completed and its niche in the church had been established.

It was within the circles of prayer-meeting people that many of the grandparents and parents of today's band members were converted. Furthermore, it was at the mourners' bench at camp meetings or prayer meetings, with the bands singing over them, that many band members of today's generation also were converted, as Mary Allen and Alfred Green describe in this book. The truth about which the bands sing—the redemptive presence of the divine spark returning once again in their midst, just as it was present with heroes of the Bible; the validation of those who are humble and genuine in spirit; and the judgment against the falsely proud—was enough to open the hearts of those who attended a camp meeting, but who otherwise might be lost.

The overwhelming power of racism and the general prejudice against things African nearly killed the ring shout. Where it did not die, it was driven underground and nearly off the pages of history. Strong traditions, however, often have a way of living on. Perhaps the invisibility of the shout to the outside world allowed it, paradoxically, to survive. Today, some younger people who were raised in the Singing and Praying Bands are taking a new pride in this tradition, in the same way that many African Americans have developed a renewed fascination with Africa and their own African roots, and in the same way Americans of all backgrounds have come to value their common cultural heritage. It is a tradition worthy of being valued.

One need not be born and raised in this tradition to value the Singing and Praying Bands. These bands have a universal relevance. Their genius is that they distill in a religious service a more general spirit of mutual aid or "help" that was the backbone of rural African American life in the upper South and mid-Atlantic region. They create a *circle of community* based on the old folk wisdom that one good turn deserves another. They give a positive slant to the proverb "what goes around comes around."

As the Singing and Praying Bands raise a hymn of repentance, the members identify their individual failings and pain with the suffering of Jesus. As they relive their experiences, they are animated by a sense of acceptance and love more powerful than tragedy. They become touched by the Spirit and imbued with a compassion for others who suffer. This spirit brings to band members an immediate sense of redemption.

The band members say that this Spirit of God "runs from heart to heart and breast to breast." This is important. It is this Spirit that Gertrude Stanley refers to metaphorically later in this volume when she says that "there must be a wheel in the middle of the wheel." This image is drawn from a vision that came to the prophet Ezekiel, recorded in Ezekiel 1:15–21. Like the phrase "from heart to heart and from breast to breast," this expression is traditional to the Singing and Praying Bands and to the larger religious movement in the nineteenth century that gave rise to the African American spirituals. An anonymous folk poet in the nineteenth century composed a song based on the text from Ezekiel. It includes these words:

Ezekiel saw the wheel, way in the middle of the air.
The big wheel runs by faith; the little wheel runs by the grace of God.
The wheel in a wheel, way in the middle of the air.[85]

When band members say that the spirit runs from heart to heart and breast to breast, they are alluding to the sacred circle of community that their service validates every time they form a circle and sing. But there is more to the community than this. There is a second wheel, in the middle of the wheel of community, as Gertrude Stanley reminds us: this is God, the abstracted ideal of love that underlies sacred human transactions. It is this idea that holds the wheel of community together.

This idea of community, as well as the immediate sense of spirit and redemption that the band members experience during their worship, is thoroughly Christian. Yet the symbolism of a circle in motion is demonstrably African in origin. Combined, these two concepts and the two symbols of the cross and the circle represent the essence of the African American worldview expressed in the spirituals. In fact, they represent one the great expressions of spirituality to come from American society. The truths thereby articulated transcend the parochial and instead approach universal relevance.

This vision implicit in African American Christianity extends beyond the concept of the ring shout. In the service of the Singing and Praying Bands, the vision within that circle of community—expressed in the imagery of the march around Jericho as well as in the vision of Ezekiel—eventually becomes so powerful and so pervasive that the participants want to take it to the world. The ring opens up, and those inside it march out into the world with this universal witness. This transition arguably turns an esoteric regional tradition into one that significantly affected larger developments in American social history. In much of the black church, the perfectly ordinary English word "march" has taken on a more specialized meaning, denoting a group walk in solidarity toward religious and political salvation. It is possible that the messianic message underlying the civil rights movement and the civil rights marches that stormed into the center of American life in the 1950s and 1960s had its origin with the ring shout, with the religious sensibility of the spirituals, and with the metaphoric march around Jericho that was common in nineteenth-century and early twentieth century black camp meetings and other religious gatherings, and that is still practiced by the Singing and Praying Bands.[86]

The nineteenth-century African American religious patterns that underlie the practice of the Singing and Praying Bands still reverberate throughout African American culture in numerous ways, several of which merit review here. First, like the Singing and Praying Bands before them, contemporary gospel choirs maintain a tradition of fellowshipping with each other. They prize the moral value given to the social and economic traditions of mutual aid that are at the root of the band tradition. Like the Singing and Praying Bands before them, gospel choirs travel together from church to church for their performances. Just as each band sponsored a yearly camp meeting at its home church, a gospel choir sponsors an annual anniversary of the founding of its own choir at its home church. Gospel choirs from churches that the host choir visited will return the favor and perform at the anniversary celebration. This tradition of mutual aid is manifest not just sociologically, in the networks of fellowshipping, but also *aesthetically*, in the call-and-response performances prevalent in gospel music. Finally, gospel choir members sing to facilitate the in-filling of the Spirit that runs from heart to heart and breast to breast through performance in ways that recall earlier traditions. The spirit of mutual aid that animated the ring shout remains alive and well.

Second, the old-time religion of the Singing and Praying Bands continues in the twenty-first century in the sanctified churches of the Holiness and Pentecostal movements. The bands have always emphasized the power of the Holy Spirit to convert sinners, transform lives, and breathe a renewed spirit into the lives of long-term believers. Beginning after the Civil War and after Emancipation, some officials of established denominations—such as the aforementioned Bishop Payne—attempted to make their churches' styles of worship more formal and restrained, while de-emphasizing the power of the Spirit of God working in its own way. It was at that time that the Holiness movement emerged out of Methodism, in an effort to retain the intense spirit of Christian perfection that had dominated early Methodism. The dawn of the twentieth century saw the birth of the related Pentecostal religious movement. Together, the Holiness and Pentecostal movements experienced phenomenal growth among African Americans during the twentieth century, in large part because these movements affirmed the power of the Holy Spirit working in the lives of the saints of the church as central to their religious practice. In some ways, then, it can be legitimately claimed that the sanctified churches are a major heir to the type of religious service that the Singing and Praying Bands maintained in the nineteenth century. In these newer churches, the bands' religious thrust persists.

Furthermore, forms of worship that resemble the ring shout continue to crop up in such lively, sanctified churches. For example, the African American dancer Katherine Dunham, employed during the Great Depression by the Federal Writers' Project, observed such services in urban sanctified churches in New York City. She recalled:

> In 1938–39, I had occasion to direct a group in the Federal Writers' Project in an investigation of religious and magic cults in the city. Here, while the ideology was clearly and definitively Christian (with added flourishes), the entire pattern of religious behavior associated with it was almost as purely African. The rhythmic percussion-type hand-clapping and foot-stamping, the jumping and leaping, the "conversion" or "confession" in unknown tongues which is a form of possession or ecstasy (induced in some cases, by a circle of "saints" or "angels" closing in upon the person in rhythmic motion of a dance), the frequent self-hypnosis by motor activity of the shoulders—all these African forms were present.[87]

Dunham is certainly only one of many to have observed such a "circle of 'saints.'" Altar services in which saints of the church come to the cross aisle and form a circle to pray, sing, and shout continue to be quite common.

Finally, the principle of circularity in ring shout traditions is present today in yet another way. For example, when members of a gospel quartet come to the center aisle of a church to perform, they will often form a line behind their designated soloist and back her up as she faces the congregation and leads it in a rousing hymn. If the performance succeeds and the congregation is moved, worshippers will, while remaining in the pews, stand up, and clap their hands and pat their feet. Those in the amen corner, to one side of the center aisle, also may stand and clap. Those standing by the musical instruments on the other side of the cross aisle will also participate. Behind the altar rail, those in the choir loft to one side of the pulpit also stand and get into the swing of things. Remaining in their positions, all will turn and face the soloist: invisible radii, like the spokes of Ezekiel's wheel, seem to connect the soloist and each member of the community. In this way, the congregation as a whole teases a circle out of the rectangle of the sanctuary and the straight lines of the pews. There—*right there*—in the most popular performance tradition in black churches today, is a hand-clapping circle, a soloist performing for the community, a common pattern of performance in many genres of African American performance. Arguably, ring shouts survive in gospel performances such as these.

This rich African American religious tradition can inform our own larger struggle for community and spirituality as we confront the juggernaut of the marketplace. One does not need to be a biblical literalist to appreciate these values. One need only understand, first, that vibrant communities are built from traditions of reciprocity among individuals, and that whatever it is that we call "holy" often is most clearly manifested in a community of people deeply engaged with each other, both in the present and historically. Such an understanding has been a major thrust of twentieth-century thought. The existential philosopher Karl Jaspers held that authenticity in existence is to be found not in any particular religious creed, but in a real engagement with the depths of life.[88] The phenomenologist Edmund Husserl taught that this engagement with life is shaped by and articulated in the circumstances of our concrete daily existence.[89] A folklorist merely needs to add that a people's deep and active engagement with life can be best discerned in its creative expressions of belief, such as in the camp meetings, songs, and prayers of the Singing and Praying Bands. In this book, a number of band members explain how their individual experiences became inseparable from this religious tradition. Their personal testimonies fit together into a narrative ensemble that describes the tradition as a whole. This tradition, so full of that wisdom born of living, cannot be objectified as something separate from the lives of those who have kept it alive. My hope is that every reader will apply some of the wisdom of the band tradition to their own lives and communities.

Notes

1. This portrait of an old-time camp meeting in the Chesapeake Bay area is something of a composite, drawn from the memories of the many participants with whom I have talked. Cordonsal Walters, interview, July 7, 1998; Benjamin Beckett, interview, May 24, 1999. Unless noted otherwise, all interviews were conducted by the author.

2. Cordonsal Walters, interview, July 7, 1998; Alfred Green, interviews, September 3 and December 22, 1995; Rev. Edward Johnson, interviews, March 19 and November 6, 1987. According to Walters, ferries used to leave from the Grey's Ferry area of Philadelphia, for example, and drop people off in Frederica, Delaware. From Frederica, those heading to the camp meetings in southern Delaware would travel by horse and wagon.

3. Alfred Green, interview, September 3, 1995; Susanna Watkins, interview, June 16, 1996.

4. Benjamin Beckett, interviews, April 14 and May 24, 1999; Rev. Edward Johnson, interview, October 14, 1986; Cordonsal Walters, interview, July 7, 1998.

5. Alfred Green, interviews, September 3, 1995, and January 3, 1996.

6. Cordonsal Walters, interview, July 7, 1998.

7. Benjamin and George Beckett, interview, August 17, 1996; George Beckett, interview, May 24, 1999; Alfred Green, interviews, September 3, 1995, and January 3, 1996. I discuss the ring shout in detail later in this introduction.

8. In referring to the Singing and Praying Bands in his autobiography as "heathenish," as an "ignorant mode of worship," and even as a "Voudoo Dance," the nineteenth-century Bishop Daniel Alexander Payne of the A.M.E. Church implies knowledge of the pre-Christian, African roots of this mode of worship and these groups. Payne, *Recollections of Seventy Years*, 253–56.

9. Michel Chevalier writes that the Methodist camp meetings were festivals attuned to the ethos of the new American democracy. Chevalier, *Society, Manners and Politics*, 306 (letter of August 7, 1835, from Bedford Springs, Pennsylvania). Two separate books, *The Frontier Camp Meeting*, by Charles A. Johnson, and *And They All Sang Hallelujah*, by Dickson D. Bruce Jr., give overviews of the history of the American camp meeting tradition. In the latter, see especially pp. 36–95.

10. Yoder, *Pennsylvania Spirituals*, 1–32.

11. W. Williams, *Garden of American Methodism*, 112 (Methodism's antislavery witness); Berlin, *Slaves without Masters*, 71 (number of black converts to Methodism), 66 (black Methodists in Virginia). According to the internal statistics of the Methodist Episcopal Church itself there were 10,859 white church members in Virginia, and 2,531 black members in Virginia in 1800, a total of 13,390 members. See *Minutes of the Methodist Conferences*, 240–41.

12. DuBois, *Negro Church*, 137–38.

13. Gutman, *Black Family*, 34.

14. Curtin, *Atlantic Slave Trade*, 156–58.

15. United States Bureau of the Census, *Negro Population in the United States, 1790–1915*, 45 (African population in Virginia and Maryland in 1790), 57 (numbers of enslaved Africans and nonslave blacks in Virginia and Maryland). Virginia had a population of 12,866 nonslave blacks and Maryland had 8,043 (ibid.). In 1790, the total African population, both enslaved and free, in the United States was 757,181; out of that total, 429,358 lived in Maryland, Delaware, and Virginia. The total enslaved population of the United States in the same year was 697,624; of these, 404,550 lived in Maryland, Delaware, and Virginia. These totals can be tallied from the numbers given in *Negro Population in the United States*, 57.

16. DuBois, *Philadelphia Negro*, 19.

17. Ibid., 221–22.

18. R. Allen, *Life Experience and Gospel Labors*, 28–31.

19. Raboteau, *Fire in the Bones*, 93.

20. Watson, *Methodist Error*, 30. In an even earlier remark—in 1804—the Methodist itinerant minister William Colbert alludes to a distinctive black religious song tradition at Bethel Church in Philadelphia, writing, "My feelings were much hurt at Dr. B's by J.W.'s satirical annimadvertions on the poor black peoples [*sic*] singing last night, or rather what they sing." Colbert, "Journal," entry for September 27, 1804.

21. Dena Epstein writes that she considers Sir Charles Lyell's description of a ring shout in coastal Georgia in 1845, found in his book *A Second Visit to the United States of North America*, to be the earliest extant written reference to a ring shout. Epstein, *Sinful Tunes and Spirituals*, 233.

22. Leedom, *Westtown under the Old and New Regime*, 170.

23. Genovese, *Roll, Jordan, Roll*, 281.

24. Raboteau, *Fire in the Bones*, 17–36 (on African American Christianity and Israelites); Genovese, *Roll, Jordan, Roll*, 254 (on Jesus and Moses).

25. Planners of Gabriel's rebellion used revival meetings as events in which to meet and organize. Nat Turner was a Baptist lay preacher as well as a prophet and seer. See Mullin, *Flight and Rebellion*, 140–63.

26. The theologian James Cone, for example, writes about African American Christianity by focusing exclusively on the lyrics of spirituals. In particular, he writes, "The divine liberation of the oppressed from slavery is the central theological concept in the black spirituals." Cone, *Spirituals and the Blues*, 34.

27. The famous spiritual "Go Down, Moses," which recounts the story of Moses leading the Israelites out of slavery, and which includes the phrase "let my people go," seems to have been most widespread in Maryland and Virginia. It first appeared in print after Rev. Lewis Lockwood heard it sung at Fortress Monroe in Virginia, in 1861. He sent a copy of the song to a YMCA official in New York City, who sent it to the *New York Tribune* on December 2, 1861. The letter accompanying the song, written by the YMCA official, Harwood Vernon, adds that "it is said to have been sung for at least fifteen or twenty years in Virginia and Maryland and in all the slave states." The same song was also recorded after an observer heard it sung at a school for black children in Washington D.C. in May 1862. Epstein, *Sinful Tunes and Spirituals*, 245–46, 250. The association of this spiritual and the role of deliverer with Harriet Tubman can be seen, for example, in the title, subtitle, and content of the early biography of Tubman by Sarah Bradford. See Bradford, *Harriet Tubman*, v–vi, 3.

28. Douglass, *My Bondage and My Freedom*, 170.

29. A white Methodist minister who described specifically African American services at biracial antebellum camp meetings on the Delmarva Peninsula relates that one of the popular verses in the African American singing of the time was, "Come, childering, storm ole Jericho's walls; yes, blow an' shout, an' down dey falls!" Todd, *Methodism of the Peninsula*, 182.

30. A map appearing in Don Yoder's excellent book *Pennsylvania Spirituals* includes today's mid-Atlantic states of New Jersey, New York, Pennsylvania, Delaware, Maryland, Virginia, and West Virginia. In it the boundaries of the Baltimore and Philadelphia Conferences of the Methodist Episcopal Churches in 1850 are outlined. The areas with a large African American population are shaded. This map can give the reader an idea of the area in which the bands arose. See Yoder, *Pennsylvania Spirituals*, ix.

31. Wesley, "Rules of the Band Societies," 77–79.

32. In the preface to their two-volume collection of spirituals, James Weldon Johnson and J. Rosamond Johnson write, for example, that after a church service, church members might whisper to others an invitation to remain in church if they wanted to participate in a service that they particularly referred to as a ring shout: "Stay after church; there's going to be a 'ring shout.'" Johnson and Johnson, *Books of American Negro Spirituals*, vol. 1, 33.

33. Lomax and Lomax, *Folksong U.S.A.*, 335. In distinction to the Lomax remarks that the

ring shout is danced to a song in a leader-chorus form, a few observers comment not on the antiphonal form, but on the repetition of a chorus. Thomas Wentworth Higginson, for example, wrote that the shouters he witnessed sang "one of their quaint, monotonous, endless negro-Methodist chants, with obscure syllables recurring constantly." Higginson, *Army Life in a Black Regiment*, 17.

34. Rev. Edward Johnson, interviews, June 1, 1988, and May 18, 1989. Narratives collected from former slaves in the twentieth century corroborate Rev. Johnson's account of ring shouts held secretly in outdoor meeting spots in the antebellum South. See, for example, "Sylvia King," in Rawick, *The American Slave*, vol. 4, pt. 2, 294, and "Wash Wilson," ibid., vol. 5, pt. 4, 197–98.

35. See Rose, *Rehearsal for Reconstruction*, for further reading about efforts to uplift the former slaves of the Sea Islands during the Civil War.

36. See, for example, Spaulding, "Under the Palmetto," 188–200; Forten, "Life on the Sea Islands," 593–94; Hale and Gannett, "Freedmen of Port Royal," 9–11; W. Allen, "Negro Dialect"; and M.R.S., "A Visitor's Account." Also, Thomas Wentworth Higginson, an officer in the Union army, wrote an article that alluded to Sea Island ring shouts; see Higginson, "Negro Spirituals."

37. Allen, Ware, and Garrison, *Slave Songs of the United States*, xiv.

38. Subsequent salient writings include Christiansen, "Spirituals and 'Shouts' of Southern Negroes"; Gordon, "Folk Songs of America"; Parrish, *Slave Songs of the Georgia Sea Islands*, 54–92; Carawan, "Spiritual Singing in the South Carolina Sea Islands"; Hawes and Jones, *Step It Down*, 125, 143–46; and Rosenbaum, *Shout Because You're Free*.

39. References to groups of singers who accompany a ring shout from the side are not uncommon. In 1867, in *The Nation*, for example, an unnamed author describes such a group of singers to the side of those shuffling around in the ring, writing, "Sometimes he dances silently, sometimes as he shuffles he sings the chorus of the spiritual, and sometimes the song itself is also sung by the dancers. But more frequently, a band, composed of some of the best singers and of tired shouters, stand at the side of the room to 'base' the others, singing the body of the song and clapping their hands together or on the knees." See "The Magazine for June." Henry George Spaulding also described such a group of singers singing to the side of a ring shout: "Three or four, standing still, clapping their hands and beating time with their feet, commence singing in unison one of the shout melodies, while the others walk round in a ring, in single file, joining also in the song." Spaulding, "Under the Palmetto," 197.

40. Concerning the choruses prevalent in the mid-Atlantic ring shout, in the early nineteenth century, for example, John Fanning Watson remarked that the songs of shouters were "lengthened out with long repetition *choruses*." Watson, *Methodist Error*, 30. Rev. Robert Todd quoted a "stanza and chorus" that is familiar to him "as an illustration" of a shout song. Todd, *Methodism of the Peninsula*, 181. Leedom remarked that the shout he and others heard at a black camp meeting near Westtown, Pennsylvania consisted of "a monotonous continuation of a few lines from a hymn." Leedom, *Westtown under the Old and New Regime*, 170.

41. Concerning the mid-Atlantic tradition in which a person leads the shout from the center of the ring, John Dixon Long wrote that "the company will then form a circle around the singer." Long, *Pictures of Slavery*. Margaret Newbold Thorpe recorded that "a circle will be formed with a man standing in the center." Thorpe, "Life in Virginia," 19–21. W. E. B. DuBois similarly commented on such a central figure, writing that the leader of the ring shout "entered the ring, and with clapping of hands and contortions led the devotions." DuBois, *Philadelphia Negro*, 220.

42. References to jumping and leaping, while not confined to the mid-Atlantic, are nonetheless common in this area. John Dixon Long wrote that shouters "form a circle around the singer, and jump and bawl to their heart's [sic] content." Long, *Pictures of Slavery*, 383. Margaret Newbold Thorpe, observing a similar shout near Yorktown, Virginia, after Emancipation,

wrote that worshippers culminated the shout by "clapping their hands, jumping about, embracing and crying." Thorpe, "Life in Virginia," 19–21. W. E. B. DuBois described participants "frequently springing into the air." DuBois, *Philadelphia Negro*, 220. Rev. Todd wrote that at antebellum camp meetings on the Eastern Shore of Maryland, the shout was concluded by "'walking, and leaping and praising the Lord.'" Todd, *Methodism of the Peninsula*, 181.

43. It would be impossible—and unnecessary—to survey the entire corpus of songs from both regions to illustrate thematic similarities in songs from the two areas. Yet concerning the examples of Gabriel and his trumpet and John on the island of Patmos, I include in this volume two songs of the Singing and Praying Bands, "Blow, Gabriel" and "He Put John on the Island." Songs of a similar theme can be found throughout the literature of shout songs and spirituals in the Deep South.

44. Johnson, *The Frontier Camp Meeting*, 81–82. An important Methodist minister who witnessed firsthand the earliest Methodist camp meetings wrote definitively in 1809 that "these meetings have never been authorized by the Methodists, either at their general or annual conferences. They have been allowed of, but we as a body of people have never made any rules or regulations about them." Lee, *Short History of the Methodists*, 362.

45. David, "On One Accord," 284–321. See also David, "The Sermon and the Shout."

46. Bernard White praying during a Singing and Praying Band service at Friendship United Methodist Church, outside of Millsboro, Delaware, October 30, 1983, and at St. Paul's United Methodist in Harrisville, Maryland August 17, 1986. White uses the same words for the invocation in the different prayers given on these different dates.

47. Bernard White praying during a Singing and Praying Band service at Jefferson United Methodist in Smithville, Maryland, June 30, 1985.

48. The association between the ring shout and funerals has long been noted. In 1887, for example, a correspondent from the *Boston Herald* wrote that in Arkansas, the congregation of an African American church "kept up fires and queer dances around the grave of their dead pastor." "Negro Dances in Arkansas." In interviews published in the Georgia Writers Project work *Drums and Shadows* several individuals describe ring shouts around the graves of the recently deceased. One person, for example, states, "In the ole days they always use tuh beat the drum at the funeral an they still does it tuhday. As they take the body tuh the graveyahd, they beat the drum as they move long. They put the body in the grave. Then they mahch roun an sing and beat the drum." Another states, "Evrybody mahch roun the grave in a succle and shout an pray." Georgia Writers Project of the Works Progress Administration, *Drums and Shadows*, 125, 127. Sarah Bradford recounts the events at a funeral that Harriet Tubman witnessed in South Carolina, writing that "the whole congregation went round in a sort of 'spiritual shuffle,'" at the end of the memorial service and then marched to the grave site. Bradford, *Harriet Tubman*, 104. Sterling Stuckey discusses at length the many meanings of the ring shout in antebellum African American culture, including burial ceremonies. Stuckey, *Slave Culture*, 3–97.

49. In this vein, W. E. B. DuBois wrote that "so completely do cultural aspects of their group efforts overshadow the economic efforts that at first a student is tempted to think that there has been no inner economic co-operation, or at least it has come to the fore in the last two or three decades. But this is not so. While to be sure the religious motive was uppermost during the time of slavery for instance, so far as group actions among the Negroes were concerned, even then it has an economic tinge, and more so since slavery, has Negro religion had its economic side." DuBois, *Economic Co-operation among Negro Americans*, 10–11.

50. In Frankford, Delaware, first-cousin marriage was not uncommon in the past, although it was not the usual practice. Also, many individuals were related to others in the community on both the maternal and paternal sides of their families. Benjamin and George Beckett, interview, July 12, 1999.

51. Information about the familial aspect of the ring shout is mostly unavailable. Neverthe-

less, in his book about the McIntosh County Shouters of coastal Georgia, Art Rosenbaum corroborates this observation, writing that all of the contemporary shouters in that group are descendants of four sisters, who were themselves "all daughters of London and Amy Jenkins." Rosenbaum, *Shout Because You're Free*, 55.

52. DuBois, *Philadelphia Negro*, 221–22.

53. Thompson, *African Art in Motion*, 28.

54. Call-and-response singing is not unique to Africa or the African diaspora. It was also common in European sacred music and in the lined-out hymns of European extraction that enslaved Africans heard and sang in formal religious services. Yet the overlapping call-and-response that Thompson refers to is a distinct form of this more pervasive phenomenon. In the African-derived pattern, the leader assumes his role only temporarily, and the group infringes on the leader's words, lending him support while limiting his authority. While Thompson writes about the African derivation of the call-and-response style of singing, Melville Herskovits asserts that the benevolent and mutual aid societies that became so important to African American culture also grew from African roots. He writes, "Cooperation among the Negroes of this society is principally found in such institutions as lodges and other benevolent societies, which in themselves are directly in tune with the tradition underlying similar African organizations." Herskovits, *Myth of the Negro Past*, 161. Tying together the two concepts—that is, the aesthetics of song and traditions of cooperative labor—Harold Courlander writes, "It is not only in group singing that the American Negro work gang shows similarities with African tradition, but in patterns of group working as well." These work patterns include, "the rhythmic use of tools, the sense of community, and responsive singing." Courlander, *Negro Folk Music U.S.A.*, 91–92. In the bands, traditions of mutual aid and the ring shout are two dimensions of the same phenomenon.

55. Thompson, *African Art in Motion*, 27–28.

56. I explored in earlier works many of the ideas regarding the larger meanings of the counterclockwise march around the mourners' bench. See David, "On One Accord: Community, Musicality, and Spirit Among the Singing and Praying Bands of Tidewater Maryland and Delaware," 236–83, and "On One Accord: Theology and Iconography of a Ring Shout."

57. "An Englishman in South Carolina," 114.

58. Johnson and Johnson, *Books of American Negro Spirituals*, 33. Other nineteenth- and early twentieth-century observers of the ring shout also commented that it seemed to be a clear African survival in North America. Thomas Higginson, a white Northerner who commanded a regiment of South Carolina freedmen during the Civil War, wrote that the hut that his soldiers built for their prayer meeting was "made neatly of palm-leaves and covered in at top, a regular native African hut." Higginson, *Army Life in a Black Regiment*, 17. Laura Towne, a teacher and nurse who worked with former slaves on the Sea Islands of South Carolina, wrote that "the shout . . . seems to me certainly the remains of some old idol worship." See Towne, *Letters and Diary of Laura M. Towne*, 20. The authors of *Slave Songs of the United States*, the first complete book to be published about the religious songs of former slaves of the South, thought "it is not unlikely that this remarkable religious ceremony is a relic of some native African dance." Allen, Ware, and Garrison, *Slave Songs of the United States*, xiv. Charlotte Forten, a schoolteacher from the famous African American Forten family of nineteenth-century Philadelphia, who taught freedmen in South Carolina during Reconstruction, concluded that shouts probably "are the barbarous expression of religion, handed down to them from their African ancestors." Forten, "Life on the Sea Islands," 594. Abigail Christiansen observed that "shouts were no doubt survivals of African dances used in fetish or idol worship." Christiansen, "Spirituals and 'Shouts' of Southern Negroes," 155. Lydia Parrish, a Quaker women from Salem County, New Jersey, and the wife of the painter Maxfield Parrish, observed ring shouts on St. Simon's Island in Georgia and wrote that "those who have traveled to Africa, and seen

native dancing, are convinced that the shout is nothing more than a survival of an African tribal dance." Parrish, *Slave Songs of the Georgia Sea Islands*, 54.

59. Lomax and Lomax, *Folksong U.S.A.*, 335.

60. Herskovits, *Myth of the Negro Past*, 215–16.

61. Raboteau, *Slave Religion*, 65–66.

62. Watson, *Annals of Philadelphia*, 483.

63. Brackett, *Negro in Maryland*, 92, 100.

64. Jones, *Religious Instruction of the Negroes*, 53, and DuBois, *Negro Church*, 19–20.

65. Colbert, "Journal," entry for December 6, 1801.

66. Robert Farris Thompson writes that in Kongo art and religion in particular, a circular "cosmogram" is often "marked on the ground for purposes of initiation and mediation of spiritual power between worlds." Further, he writes that singing and "tracing in appropriate media the ritually designated 'point' or 'mark' of contact will result in the descent of God's power upon that very point." He maintains also that this cosmogram tradition survived in the New World as *"singing and drawing points of contact between worlds."* Thompson, *Flash of the Spirit*, 108, 110.

67. Herskovits's theory is that "the most striking and recognizable survivals of African religion are in those behavioristic aspects that, given overt expression, are susceptible of reinterpretation in terms of a new theology while retaining their older established forms." Herskovits, *Myth of the Negro Past*, 214.

68. David, "The Sermon and the Shout."

69. Todd, *Methodism of the Peninsula*, 81.

70. Payne, *Recollections of Seventy Years*, 81.

71. Ibid., 256.

72. Colbert, "Journal," entry for August 26, 1804.

73. Watson, *Methodist Error*, 23n.

74. Long, *Pictures of Slavery*, 383.

75. DuBois, *Philadelphia Negro*, 220–21.

76. Bennett, *Memorials of Methodism*, 569–70.

77. Leedom, *Westtown under the Old and New Regime*, 170.

78. Watson, *Methodist Error*, 30–31.

79. Kephart, *Biography of Jacob Smith Kessler*, 73–74.

80. Todd, *Methodism of the Peninsula*, 179–82.

81. Steward, *Fifty Years in the Gospel Ministry*, 151–53.

82. Payne, *Recollections of Seventy Years*, 253–55.

83. Raboteau, *Fire in the Bones*, 190.

84. For the clearest statement of the complex and often tense relation between folk religions and institutional religions to which congregants give their official allegiance, see Yoder, "Toward a Definition of Folk Religion."

85. *Songs of Zion*, 84–85. I have reproduced the lyrics of this song as they are presented in this book, except I have revised the lyrics into standard English.

86. In addition to Rev. Robert Todd, other writers associate the ring shout with the extended marching that often concludes camp meetings. Such associations between the shout and the final march lend credence to the idea that the religious march was the inheritor of the shout tradition. A young Mormon missionary, James Henry Moyle, for example, described in his journal such a confluence between the two phenomena at an African American camp meeting in North Carolina in 1881: "Tuesday 13 Sept being last day of meeting they march, so we waited for that. They had kept up their shouting all night but in the morning in and out between 9 and ten oclock they all congregated or as many as they could get together and commenced their meeting or march. . . . All spred out for a march double file marched arround [*sic*] camp-

ground then in single file all singing all the time. Then they got the sinners into the center and they marched round and round with christians on outside forming two rings both as close together as possible. Sinners continued to draw closer and close until by singing &c much excitement was worked up." Extract from the diary of John Moyle, a Mormon missionary in North Carolina, quoted in Sessions, "Camp Meeting at Willow Tree, 1881." Howard Odum and Guy Johnson also associate the shout with a tradition of religious marching in church. As they write, "The church needed some kind of substitute for rhythm and excitement of the dance that would satisfy and still be 'in the Lord.' Consequently marching services were often instituted. . . . Sometimes they marched two by two . . . sometimes they marched singly, and at other times they marched in a general 'mix-up.' . . . The Negroes often imagined themselves to be the children of Israel, while their marching songs represented Moses leading them out from under the bondage of Pharaoh, or they considered themselves as marching around the wall of some besieged city. Victory would be theirs sooner or later." Odum and Johnson, *The Negro and His Songs*, 34. In one of her novels, Zora Neale Hurston includes a description of a religious "grand march" that approached secular dancing but was slightly more restrained. Hurston, *Jonah's Gourd Vine*, 114

87. Dunham, "The Negro Dance," 994.

88. Stumpf, *Socrates to Sartre*, 464. Jaspers assumes the reality of an empirical world exterior to human consciousness. This means that in the philosophy of Jaspers, the individual comes into his or her own Cartesian consciousness as an embodied person in a larger world. The conscious individual's struggle for transcendence and authenticity is informed by a deep, ongoing engagement with the specifics of his or her own life in this empirical world, rather than with any particular belief system. See Blackham, *Six Existentialist Thinkers*, 43–65.

89. Husserl's philosophy begins with his famous "phenomenological reduction," through which he sets aside epistemological, ontological, and metaphysical presuppositions to posit instead perceived phenomena as psychological facts. Subsequently, he posits that for every psychological phenomenon there is a corresponding pure phenomenon. He then takes these pure phenomena—without ever examining their ultimate reality—which form deeply contextual organic webs of meaning, as the basis of his philosophical inquiry. Husserl, *Idea of Phenomenology*, 33–34.

ONE

Alfred Green
(1908–2003)

That was a great day in my life.

I WAS AROUND ABOUT FIFTEEN years old when I was converted. In spite of going to church, I was saying and doing everything that I wanted to do. But my mother and father used to tell me, "When you get to be twelve years old, your sin is on yourself." Your sin is on them until you get to be twelve years old.

It happened at the Magothy camp meeting. It was early in the morning; it was Monday morning when the camp breaks up. A whole lot of us young boys went to the mourners' bench. They were all getting up and leaving me kneeling down there. The Singing and Praying Bands were singing over me. The devil told me to spit on my hand and rub my eyes and make out like I was crying.

And I got up to go, and an old woman named Cousin Rachel grabbed hold of my coat tail, and told me, "Come on back, Alfred, you ain't got nothing." But how did she know that? "You sit down there till the Lord blesses you."

I went back. I don't know what happened then. When I came up from the mourners' bench then, I came up shouting. I was just the same as a crazy man. They were trying to hold me down.

Old Man Pratt said, "Turn him loose, you can't hold Jesus."

I was pulling them down just like somebody was knocking them down. But I didn't mean it: I was in the Spirit.

It was such a good feeling. It was the Spirit; it was him. All I know, I could look at those old people, and there must have been a skin come over my eyes. It looked like those old people were dancing on smoke, I mean singing on a cloud. They had on those old bonnets, old long gingham aprons, old long dresses. All I can remember, the floor was down here and they were up on a cloud. That was a great day in my life. After that, I got religion, and the Spirit always has dwelled with me.

A camp meeting is something like a revival, and its purpose is to save souls. The camp meeting at my church—Mt. Zion United Methodist in Magothy, Maryland—starts on the last Sunday in August and breaks up on the first Sunday in September. Many black Methodist churches up and down the Eastern Shore and Western Shore of Maryland had camp meetings, but Magothy camp was the biggest because we stayed open every weeknight until 12:00 P.M. Then, on the last Sunday one of the Singing and Praying Bands would sing in the church after the morning preaching, and that band would march out of the church at about 3:00 P.M. And from that time on there would be different bands singing indoors and outdoors, all night long. We would sing in the church and on the grounds all night long until 12:00 noon on Monday

"The Spirit has been coming on me ever since I touched the land of Eden." Alfred Green testifies at a camp meeting at Union Wesley United Methodist Church in Clarksville, Delaware.

morning, Labor Day. Other churches would not stay open all night long like this. Most people had Labor Day off, I guess.

The Singing and Praying Bands grew out of the Methodist prayer meetings. The church members who attended prayer meetings were the people who were the most dedicated. They were the people who weren't fussing; they supported each other. Way back in the old days, in the first half of this century, when prayer meeting people didn't have anything to travel for, they'd just have prayer meetings in their own churches. They wouldn't go to any other churches.

Then after a while, they commenced meeting together. Maybe Mr. Levi Stewart from Christ Methodist in Baltimore, or another captain from the Eastern Shore, would say, "Why not come to *my* church? We have *meetings;* we have a *good* time."

That's how it spread abroad. When people in the different prayer meeting groups began to travel as a group, they called themselves the Singing and Praying Bands. Since then, all the Singing and Praying Bands have all come together for camp. So that is the purpose of our camp meetings. And the main thing is trying to save souls. All of the people that I know who got religion, got it from the Singing and Praying Bands. Of all the different church groups, they had the most spiritual power.

In the past, every church had its own band. And every band had around about forty members. Some of them had more than that. Today, all these churches from the Western Shore and Eastern Shore have enough members to make just one band. Sometimes when we all get together at a camp, we have two groups, the Western Shore band and the Eastern Shore band. But that's all there is to the bands now. When you see *all* the band members from *all* the churches singing together as a band now, that is the way *one* band was in the past.

The leaders of the Singing and Praying Bands are called band captains. The other members would follow him as a group. The captains would tell their members where and when—to which church, to which camp meeting—they were supposed to go. The captain is supposed to lead the band in the prayer service; he can lead with his hymn, or he can call on anybody he wants in his band to lead. Also, the band captain would be the chairman of his church's camp meeting. As the captain of my church's Singing and Praying Band, I run the camp. Before me was Mr. Alexander Hall, and before him, Mr. Josh Kelly. The ministers do not plan the camp meetings, and the Methodist Conferences would not have anything to do with them either; they would not care one way or another. So without the Singing and Praying Bands, there would be no camp meetings.

At Magothy camp, people would come all through the week to the camp meeting, and they would go back home at night. But they started coming in on the last Saturday night for the last Sunday. Then that last day, all the bands from all the different churches came and sang on Sunday afternoon and night, and they'd sing from the Sunday night until Monday morning.

The people from Baltimore would come on a steamboat to a place called Head of the Creek on the Stoney Creek. The steamboat would come down there three times a day, and every time she came, she was loaded.

The captain at Magothy would tell anybody who had a horse and wagon, "The boat's coming at two o'clock, and such-and-such a band will be on there and you have got to go down there and get them."

Mr. Josh Kelly, Old Man Pinckett, a whole lot of them used to drive down and pick up twenty people in each wagon. Some of them would not wait for the wagon; they would walk up to the campground. You could see them marching. Sometimes, some of the old people would start a hymn while they marched along, so that when they got on the church grounds, things would be hot. They would be in the Spirit.

They had a great big, old barbed-wire fence around the campground. And there were two gates, one on the east end and one on the west end of the grounds. They used to give out tickets for admission, and the tickets cost ten cents to come in the gate on the last day. Now Mr. Alexander Hall, who was band captain before me, had the receipts of all those who used to come in at the gate. And he would add them all up and sometimes there were over five or six thousand people who had come in. (And you know there were more than that because some used to come over the barbed-wire fence to avoid paying the admission, and you could barely squeeze through the crowds on the last day.) That was from the 1930s all the way through to the 1960s. If you were out on the grounds dining in those days, and if you told me to stay here until you came back, you couldn't find me, there were so many people.

The Magothy campground is about five acres. There was the church in the middle, and behind the church was a concession stand where they sold candy and cake, and ice cream. They had a separate old hall behind the church and to the west, near where an old hand pump used to be. Then they built a schoolhouse to the east of the church. (Now, they have turned the schoolhouse into a new hall and have torn down the old hall.) They had an outhouse for the women way down there in the woods, and one for the men down behind the old hall. They would park buggies like they park cars now. Then they would unhook the horses. They had a long pole that they would tie the horses to in the back of the church, leading toward the new hall. They had a number of horses tied there, and they put hay down on the ground and the horses would eat.

For camp meeting, they had about ten tents, and all of them were lined right up, all the way from the old hall up to the new hall, behind the church. And in front of the church, in between the church and the new hall, they had four or five tents. And vendors used to rent the tents to cook in. The vendors would sell fish, chicken, pig tails, and cabbage. And you could go in the tents and eat. They had watermelon stands. They had picture stands to take your picture.

One old woman used to have a whole lot of books she used to come down here and sell. And one old doctor—they called him the Indian doctor—used to give out different kinds of oil, snake oil and all that kind of thing. (It was good, too, for sprains and strains.) And there was a man from Philadelphia, with an old dummy, who would

Children line up in front of Henry's Photo Stand to document their presence at Mt. Zion's 139th annual camp meeting in 1997.

throw his voice around and play tricks. The vendors would be there the whole week, and they'd pay the church to have the stand.

The tents were white, and they had a fly at the back and they were open in the front. They had sides that went to the ground and they had a fly over the top, in case of rain. The tents were long and narrow. The cooking would be in the back and the eating would be up front. Some of them had three tables. My mother used to have a tent in the late 1930s. She sold pig feet, cabbage, potato soup, and she gave you bread and an ear of corn with dinner, and then coffee for free. Everything was supposed to be ready for the last Sunday in camp, so she would set up the week before camp.

Now, the people who came in from New Jersey were kind of slick. One time they had a little stand in front of the church. And they had a man who played three-card monte. But the man who was playing these cards, Paralyzed Slim, they called him, was crippled. The preacher came there; otherwise I don't think he would have known what was going on.

And Paralyzed Slim told the preacher, "You can play, too. Sometimes the devil himself don't know where the right card is."

The preacher went into the church and called up the police and a policeman came and took him out in his arms.

And there also would be a group out in the woods as thick as gnats. They had

Inside a temporary eatery at the camp meeting in Magothy, Maryland, two chefs proudly display food they have prepared to sell to those who attend.

plenty of whiskey and they would shoot craps and would be carrying on, but they stayed in the woods; they didn't come up onto the church grounds.

But you might see somebody come along with a suitcase and he would ask you, "You want to see a doctor?" Well, he would have whiskey in that suitcase. (And I imagine there were a lot of babies begot around there too.)

And the last day all the bands from all over, as far as I can remember, would come. On the last Sunday, a band would start singing in the church after the morning preaching service. And then we would come out of church around 3:00 P.M., and we'd sing all night long. Preaching would be going on in the church, and class meeting would be going on in the church, and the different bands would still be singing outdoors and marching around. And every band had about thirty or forty members.

They would have a mourners' bench in the church, pushed back next to the pews. When the band came in, they moved it out in front of the pulpit. It was about fourteen feet long. It was for the bands to sing around and for mourners to kneel beside. That's where mourners would go down and confess to the Lord. The men in the band would stand on one side of the bench and the women on the other. That's the way they would stand as they sang, hymns like "When Jesus Walked upon the Earth Some Said He Was a Spy," and "It's Jesus Christ I Long to Find, Pray Tell Me Where Is He."

With Joseph Spicer (center) leading, the bands begin to raise a hymn, the men on one side of a mourners' bench, the women facing them.

A band will start a hymn at a low pitch and slow tempo, and gradually they work it up; they go higher and higher. So they build it up, build up the Spirit, build it up in the Spirit. And they wake up to the Spirit. The Spirit gets in them. When the Spirit gets in them, you see a whole lot of them around there crying. And they pray. After a hymn, they go down in prayer. They are praying, praying, praying. Praying until something happens, until they get happy.

1. "When Jesus Walked upon the Earth"

A Give-out Hymn

The musical notation below is based on a recording of a performance of the Eastern and Western Shore Singing and Praying Bands at John Wesley United Methodist Church in Liner's Road, Dorchester County, Maryland, on June 8, 1996. Wilton Jennings of Asbury Town Neck United Methodist Church in Severna Park, Maryland, led the performance. At the beginning of the singing, the tonic was F above middle C and the tempo was 50 quarter notes per minute. At the conclusion of the performance, the tonic had risen to B above middle C, and the tempo had increased to 144 quarter notes per minute.

This hymn seems to be one of the type that the band members refer to as a "ballad hymn." Composed in America and often disseminated at camp meetings and revivals, such a hymn is usually not found in the hymnals of mainstream denominations and can usefully be referred to as a folk hymn. In this book, Alfred Green, Benjamin Beckett, and Susanna Watkins all refer to vendors who came to camp meetings and sold texts of these ballad hymns printed on pieces of paper or in slim paperback songbooks. The second verse of this hymn is similar to text from the traditional song "Savior, Don't Pass Me By."

The tune to which the bands used to sing this hymn is common in the band tradition. It can be used also to give out "Hark from the Tomb a Doleful Sound," "Am I a Soldier of the Cross," and "I Dreamed of the Great Judgment Morning."

VERSES:

2. As he passed by a sinful crowd, he heard a woman cry,
"If I could but his garment touch, I'd go down and prophesy."

3. As he turned about to see, he heard a sinner cry,
"Woman, thy faith has made me whole, go down and prophesy."

4. He spoke to Peter, James, and John, "It is written I must die.
Go shed my blood on Calvary, no more to bleed and die."

5. He called old Lazarus from the grave, while many men stood by,
"Go loose the man and set him free, that he might prophesy."

6. Oh weeping Mary came to see our loving Lord and Savior.
The angel said, "He is not here; he's gone to Galilee."

2. "It's Jesus Christ I Long to Find"

A Give-out Hymn

James Cromwell of Bethel A.M.E. Church in Cambridge, Maryland, led the Eastern and Western Shore Singing and Praying Bands in the following hymn at Williams A.M.E. Church of Newark, Worcester County, Maryland, on November 23, 1986. Williams A.M.E. is the home church of the Tindleys, the family into which Dr. Charles Albert Tindley, the famous minister and composer, was born. The performance began with E below middle C as the tonic, at a tempo of 20 quarter notes per minute. At the conclusion of the performance, the tonic had risen to A below middle C and the tempo had increased to 110 quarter notes per minute. The pitch of the third (B) varies between the minor and natural third, as does the pitch of the sixth (E). The text of the hymn ends with verse 4 below. The leader of this performance added verses 5 and 6, which come from a different source, so that the bands could continue raising the hymn and singing the last line of verse 6 over and over, in an exuberant, chanted meditation characteristic of the conclusion of band performances of such give-out hymns.

A version of this hymn appears in Newman I. White's *American Negro Folk-Songs*, pp. 123–24, under the title "Redeemed." Another version appears in White's edited work *The*

Frank C. Brown Collection of North Carolina Folklore, volume 3, p. 643. The famous gospel singer Marion Williams recorded a somewhat different version of this song, entitled "The Man I'm Looking For," on her album *I've Come So Far*, Spirit Feel Records 1002, published in 1986.

science peace. - It's - him - my - con - science peace.

Hand clapping

Foot patting

VERSES:

2. If you go down in yonder fold and search among the sheep,
You'll find him there, so I am told, with those he loves to keep.

3. What signal shall I tell him by from any other man?
He wears salvation on his brow and in his arms a lamb.

4. Thank you, kind friend, for your advice, I'll find him if I can,
And if I do I shall rejoice, for Christ is a friend to man.

5. Kind friends, I'll bid you all adieu, I'll leave you in God's care,
And if I never more see you, go on I'll meet you there.

6. He spoke to Peter, James, and John, it is written I must die.
Go shed my blood on Calvary, no more to bleed and die.

Sometimes when the band gets to singing and it sounds so good, that's when the sinners used to come in. In the past, that bench would be lined up with people kneeling down there telling the Lord to save them, what could they do to be saved, "have mercy, my Lord," "save me right now, my Lord." During the camp, there would be a line of mourners kneeling on one side of the bench and a line of mourners on the other side. And no sooner did they get up, another line would come; no sooner *they* get up, *another* line come in. They'd be converted—they would feel the Spirit for the first time—and they'd get up and shout and go on out. Those old people had power.

And when they got done singing they would "march around Jericho." They would march around the mourners' bench and march out of the church. They would march around the mourners' bench one or two times—always turning around to the right, turning around to the right—and then they would march out.

Sometimes a band would be in the church singing and praying, and another band would be outdoors, and they would want to come in and pray. And Mr. Les Green had a horn—like a foghorn—that he would blow to keep the bands from running

Rev. Bernard White kneels at the mourners' bench at Magothy, Maryland, and leads members of the Western Shore Band in a soul-stirring prayer.

into one another. And he would have to let one band know that another band was in the church praying. He stood on the steps of the church, and if a band would be coming up, he would blow the horn to let them know what to do. If there was no band in the church, he would not blow; they could march on in. If one band was in church, he'd blow *one time* to let them know there was already one in church. Then when that band would come outdoors, he would blow *two times* to let the other band know they could come on back, there was now no one in the church.

When the band marched out, they would go down to the old hall, and sing in that old hall for those who were cooking and eating in there.

And there was a well sitting in the middle of the grounds, between the church and the hall. Old Man Parker used to sit down at the well and pump the pump. (Kids would come there, you see, and they would play in the water, so someone had to stay there and watch it.) He had about five or six tin cups hanging around there. And the bands would go down there and sing around him. Then they would come up again and go back into the church to sing.

All of the bands would sing all night long. They would start after the midnight preaching, and they'd sing until Monday afternoon. They would go until the camp broke up. All the bands were singing separately: one would be singing over here, one singing over there, and one singing over there.

There was one band from Butlertown, in Kent County, on the Eastern Shore. The only man I remember was Old Man Walker. They would *never* come into the

As band captains have done since the nineteenth century, Alfred Green blows an old horn to announce the beginning of another service at Mt. Zion's camp meeting.

With Shawn Copeland leading the way, members of the Western Shore Singing and Praying Band march exuberantly between a chartered bus and two vendors' tents on Magothy's campground.

church to sing. No matter what was going on inside, they would be outside, singing. When they sang, they'd have their coats and things spread down on the ground and they would sing around them. They had their coats and hats all in the middle of their ring, and of course they would also kneel down and pray. And all of them from that band would sing all night long. They would start after midnight preaching and they'd go on until 2:00 P.M. Monday. They would go until camp broke up.

Before the church had electricity, the trustees built fire stands to provide light for the entire campground. The fire stands were square, about four feet long and four feet wide, and they had four poles put down in the ground, and they would split logs in half and lay them flat side up across the top. They would be about as high as a table, maybe higher, about four feet high. And they put some sand or dirt on top of the wood, about four inches of it, so a fire wouldn't burn the stand down.

Then they sent us boys into the woods. We used to take an old cart and go down into the woods and we'd get a whole lot of lightwood stumps. We would start a long time before camp. There used to be a place where a whole lot of trees had died, or people had cut the trees down, and we'd dig those pine stumps out of the ground, and we'd bring them up to the church and pile them up around the tents. It was hard work, but that's the only light we had.

The Singing and Praying Bands march from the church to the fellowship hall, where they form a circle and sing for those who are cooking or dining there.

An army of men from the Singing and Praying Bands leads the march around Jericho on Magothy campground.

They kept the fires going all night long. Each stump would burn about an hour, and those pine stumps burned because they had so much juice in them. You could take a match and light them, they were so dry.

At about 6:00 A.M. on the last Monday morning, all the bands lined up together for a final grand march. When they got ready to take that grand march, all the bands would line up right behind each other, about five feet apart. And Old Man Les Green would blow the horn and lead them all through the tents. They called it marching around Jericho. They were like Joshua tearing down the walls of Jericho, only they were tearing down the walls of sin around the hearts of sinners, so that the sinners would get converted.

That's how I got converted, with the Singing and Praying Bands singing over me at Magothy Church at camp meeting time, that Monday morning.

I had a whole lot of friends I used to run around with. And see, like I said, all of them went down to the mourners' bench, and all of them got up and left me down there. I saw them getting up, and I said to myself, "I must not be doing something right." So I spit on my hand and rubbed my eyes, and got up.

"Come on back," Cousin Rachel said, "Come on back, Alfred."

And I'm glad that old woman was watching me. I never felt so good in all the days of my life as when I got up from there. Sometimes I feel good like that now. The Spirit has been coming on me ever since I touched the land of Eden. I tell them, "The Lord is blessing me; he's blessing me."

Yes, it *was* a great day. A whole lot of people got saved here. Most all of the people you hear talk about got religion down at Magothy.

I hear them say that: "I got saved down at Magothy. I got saved down at Magothy." That church saved more souls than I ever knew anybody else's church to do.

TWO

Mary Allen
(b. 1925)

After you got converted, you had something you could tell.

AT MY CHURCH—St. Luke United Methodist Church, on the corner of Gilmore and Riggs Avenue, in northwest Baltimore—Oscar Johnson and I and the other band members organize the camp meeting. We call a meeting, and we decide what minister we want. And we call and see if we can get him. If he's busy, we have to get somebody else. But *we* decide, the band; that's the way it has always been.

At the camp meeting, after the guest preacher has preached, the minister of the church has his remarks. And then he'll say, "Now, I'll turn it over to the band captain."

Everybody knows they're getting ready for the collection. And the band captain gets up and calls all captains, and all captains go up. They'll ask for two women to hold the plate for the speaker. And then we start the procession for the collection.

After the collection, they call in the bands to sing. They'll have either a bench or a line of chairs in front of the pulpit, between the pews and the pulpit.

The captain will call a band to lead off and he'll say, "All other bands follow." "Follow" means "line up behind." If they call St. Luke and say, "All other bands follow," all the rest of the bands get up and line up behind St. Luke. Sometimes there are two or three rows of them.

At one time, every band was on the program, and they would call every band that was on the program for that time, "St. Luke is going to open up and Asbury-Annapolis is going to follow them, and Marley Neck is going to follow them," and on down the line. St. Luke would just line up and Asbury-Annapolis lined up behind us, and Marley Neck behind them. (Sometimes there were so many bands, if the pews weren't nailed down, they had to move them out of the way.) The St. Luke band would raise a hymn. When we finished singing that hymn, we just backed back to the back row so that all the other bands would be in front of us, and we pushed Asbury-Annapolis in. Asbury-Annapolis would come to the front. And they would go down in prayer. And if they took the prayer, they would want a third band to come up and take the next hymn.

Now they just say, "St. Luke is going to open up, and the rest of the bands fall in," in any order. "Fall in" means the same thing as "line up behind us."

The men stand behind the chairs. Their backs are to the pulpit. The men are facing the congregation. The women line up in front of the men; their backs are to the congregation. When they call St. Luke, my captain will let me know if I'm going to sing or if he's going to sing. If I've got to sing, I'm supposed to be right in the middle of all the sisters. And all my sisters of St. Luke will line up on each side of me. And Oscar Johnson is my captain, and he'll line up in front of me on the other side of the bench with his back to the pulpit.

We always had three women's captains, three men's captains, a father, and a mother. Oscar is the first captain on the men's side, and I am the first captain on the women's side. And then we had a second captain. And whoever the second men's captain is, the second women's captain is supposed to stand in front of him. If I'm in the middle, and I'm first captain, my second captain is on one side of me and my third captain is on the other side. And the mother is on one side or the other of them, even with the father. The mother of the band is supposed to see that all the sisters are lined up right. And if you're in the center and you can't raise the hymn, then the mother had the privilege of coming up and moving you out and putting someone there that could sing that hymn.

Years back, they never started a Singing and Praying Band service with a straight hymn, like "He Put John on the Island, I, John, Saw." You can do more in opening a band service with a give-out hymn than you can with a straight hymn. A give-out hymn is when you have to throw up your hands and stop and give out (or line out) the next verse. Like "Amazing Grace" in the hymnal, they have so many verses that

Raising his arms like the conductor of an orchestra, Joseph Spicer leads the Western Shore Band in a give-out hymn.

some band members don't know them. ("I Dreamed of the Great Judgment Morning" has nine verses.) That's why you line it out. We say "give it out."

For instance, if Oscar tells me to sing, he knows I am going to sing, "I am a soldier bound for glory." (My father used to be a minister, and he had his own church, and his own band. And the captain of this band, Bob Branch —he's dead now—taught me that hymn. It might have been in an old hymnal, but I learned it from him.) And then I'll start out by *saying*, "I am a soldier bound for glory, I'm a soldier going home," to let all of the other band members know what I'm singing.

3. "I'm a Soldier Bound for Glory"

A Give-out Hymn

The notation below is based on a recording of this hymn sung by the Eastern and Western Shore Singing and Praying Bands at St. Paul A.M.E. Zion, in Salisbury, Maryland, in October 1996, led by Mary Allen, of St. Luke United Methodist Church in Baltimore. The text was written by the nineteenth-century hymnist Richard Jukes (1804–67). This hymn can still be found today in *The Song Book of the Salvation Army*. The performance began at a tempo of 40 quarter notes per minute, in a key of E-flat major/C minor. The tempo and pitch rose steadily throughout the performance, peaking at 72 quarter notes per minute and ending in C major/A minor.

When performing this give-out hymn, the bands repeat the last line, "You have got to stand in judgment, just to hear what Jesus say," over and over, as a meditation, changing the melody slightly to accentuate its rhythm, and to prevent the bands from raising the pitch of the piece any further. Although they sing in unison, each individual adds her or his ornamentation to the basic tune, giving the singing a dynamic, complicated quality impossible to reproduce in notation.

love - the Sa - vior - come - come.

Hand clapping

Foot patting

VERSES:

2. When I first commenced this warfare, many said I'd run away,
But they all have been deceived, in this fight I am to stay.

3. I love Jesus, hallelujah. I love Jesus, yes I do.
I love Jesus, he's my savior. Jesus smiles and loves me too.

4. Though this world seems dark and dreary, and it's stormy in the way.
You have got to stand in judgment, just to hear what Jesus say.

The whole band usually *sings* the first verse two times and then you stop.

And then I throw up my hands and put in the next verse, "Come and hear me tell the story, all who love the Savior, come." You try to give it out—to chant it—in the same tune as you're singing it in.

They sing that twice.

And sometimes we say "'peat!" That means "go over that line again," because they don't have the tune right. Or sometimes it sounds *good* and it's so good, we say "'peat!" to sing it again.

And then I'll throw up my hands for the third verse. You're not supposed to start off running with a hymn. You're supposed to sing it and work it up and give it out according to your feelings. You start off slowly and then you raise it up. We kind of work our hymns up. They get faster, according to the Spirit. I give it out like that until the last verse.

And the last verse would be, in my hymn, "Though this world seems dark and dreary and it's stormy on the way . . ."

And then they'd sing that.

And I'll say, "You have got to stand in judgment, just to hear what Jesus say."

And when they start singing that, I'll say, "Keep it!" And that means "I'm not putting any more verses in." We want to keep going over and over the last line, because after a certain length of time, it's *good*. We want to keep it because it's *good*. They've got in the spirit, and got the swing of the hymn. When everything is going smoothly, that's when it gets *good*, when they're all singing together.

Of course, everybody has their own motion. But it seems like all the band people have the same motion; you see us all swaying the same way, and coming back the same way. And the band people and some of the people in their seats are clapping. That's as much a part of the band as the singing; otherwise, we could sit down and sing. When it has started getting *good*, they whoop and shout and cry. (But back then when we had some great bands, it was *really pretty*.)

Then you're ready to go down on your knees in prayer. Back in those days, all men had white handkerchiefs. And if my band went down in prayer, Oscar would take his handkerchief and hit me on the shoulder and that was a sign for me to do the next thing, to pray. The captain knew those who could sing and those who could pray. The captains knew their sheep back in those years.

Some of them *really pray*, now. Some of them can really spin it out, praying whatever is on their hearts, I'm telling you. Most of us came up through the mourners' bench, you see. And that makes a difference, when you've got to stay at the mourners' bench until you are converted. It seems like it has a different effect on you than people just growing up and joining the church.

I got converted when I was ten years old. They were running a revival at my father's church, Trinity U.C.M.E., on the 900 block of West Saratoga Street. When other

"When it has started getting *good*, they whoop and shout and cry," says Mary Allen. Everyone is in motion as a shout breaks out among the Singing and Praying Bands.

people were dancing and going to movies, I was sitting in some holy, sanctified church. I didn't care what kind of church it was, but I always liked to go to church. So this revival started on a Sunday and it ended on a Sunday. On the ending Sunday, when whoever was preaching for the revival extended the invitation, I went up and told him that I wanted to join the church.

So they told me they were glad to have me, but I would have to go to the mourners' bench. As soon as you opened any church door, that's the first thing that met your eyes. That's the first thing you saw because it sat across the rostrum. Sunday after Sunday, the mourners' bench stayed right across the pulpit.

They told me I would have to go to the mourners' bench.

So I told them, "Okay."

And they were going to extend the revival another week. So I asked them, "Should I come back every night?"

They said, "Yeah."

So I came back every night, Monday night down to Friday, and I went to that mourners' bench, and the Singing and Praying Bands sang over me. And the old ones would lean over my shoulder and tell me to ask the Lord to have mercy on my soul.

And every time I would say that, they would say, "Yes, Lord!"

And then that Friday night, I went down to that mourners' bench. I remember going down, but I don't remember coming up. When I came to myself, I was crying and shouting and rejoicing in the Lord, because I had been converted. That's when God separates sin from your soul.

Then after I got myself straightened out, I had to get up from where I was sitting, and turn around and face the church people and tell them what the Lord had done for me.

And then, after that, the minister, who was my father, Rev. Walter H. Sewell, told me that I couldn't join the church yet. I would be put on probation. And if I ran well and did the things pleasing in the sight of the church and God, I would be ready after six months. So that's what happened.

Yes, after you got converted, you had something you could tell. So, a prayer is whatever comes from your heart, whatever is laid on your heart to say. Most of the time they begin a prayer with a hymn text. Most of the time, you don't know you are going to be called on. You just have to be ready (or try to be ready, anyway). I mean, you are not thinking about praying, and you go there and kneel for a few minutes and then something will come into your heart to start off with. Starting off with a hymn will get you in the mood, because it's something they know. Sometimes you just start off, "Lord, I'm down here and I'm leaning on you. I can't do nothing till you come."

And we study the Bible, and we know what's in the Bible. So sometimes the praying person has been through something you might not know about, and they'll say, "You

"A prayer is whatever comes from your heart, whatever is laid on your heart to say." Mary Allen first kneels and then walks the aisle during her prayer at a camp meeting on Taylors Island, Dorchester County, Maryland.

are the same God that heard Daniel in the lion's den, and the three Hebrew boys in the fiery furnace (he did bring them through) . . . and you heard me one day."

So God can bring them through whatever situation they are in. (When I was converted, he heard me that Friday night.)

And you want the Spirit to come, so that's what you tell him. You can use this as an invocation: "Savior, Savior, hear my humble cry; whilst on others thou art calling, do not pass me by."

And then, the people in the church, or the ones kneeling around whoever is praying, say to "tell God what you want." If you are weak, tell him "thou art mighty," and to hold you with his powerful hand.

A lot of them might say, "Bless my children that are out of the arc of safety." "Out of the arc of safety" means that they are not in the church.

Those are old prayers. That's how old people used to pray, but that's how the Singing and Praying Bands still pray.

We try to sing two give-out hymns and get in two prayers—at least two—before we sing a straight hymn. You always sing a straight hymn when you are getting ready to close the service and march. A straight hymn doesn't have any verses. A straight hymn is when you sing the same three- or four line chorus over and over again:

> We will never grow old—
> We will never grow old.
> We're going to a land
> Where we'll never grow old!

A straight hymn works its way up to certain level; it doesn't take as long as a give-out hymn. You start out slow and work it up a little bit faster, and to a little bit higher pitch. You sing that chorus through at least three times.

And then whoever is leading the hymn will put a verse in, Or if the leader wants somebody else to put a verse in, he'll say, really low, "You take it," or "Put a verse in there." Most of the verses have two lines, as far as I know. Like you would say, "Let's go see, let's go see . . ." And the next line would be, "Let's go see what the end will be."

At one time, they might tell you, "No, that verse doesn't go in that hymn," but now you can put any verse in any hymn. Most of the verses come from the Bible, and most of them rhyme, like: "Mary came running, what did she cry? / 'If thou had a-been here, our brother wouldn't have died.'" The verses are not rhymed in the Bible; our parents and the bands before took the Bible verses and rhymed them like that.

And so they will *sing:*

> We will never grow old—
> We will never grow old.
> We're going to a land
> Where we'll never grow old!

Then they will put in the first line of the verse, and then you sing the last line of the straight hymn:

> Let's go see; let's go see . . .
> Going to a land where we'll never grow old!

And we sing that. And then:

> Let's go see what the end will be.
> Going to a land where we'll never grow old!

And then we go back to singing "We will never grow old" and repeat the whole chorus. Sometimes they repeat that verse again; sometimes they don't. Then they put in another verse. You just throw up your hands, and put in the next verse:

> Mary came running, what did she cry . . .
> Going to a land where we'll never grow old!

And then you say:

> "If Thou had a-been here, our brother wouldn't have died."
> Going to a land where we'll never grow old!

4. "We Will Never Grow Old"

A Straight Hymn

The notation below is based on a version of this song that the Singing and Praying Bands sang at Malone United Methodist Church in Madison, Maryland, on September 14, 1986, with Catherine Ennels leading. Like almost all band pieces, it begins slowly, at 72 quarter notes per minute, and slowly increases in tempo, to 160 per minute. The tonic also rises during the course of the singing, from F below middle C to C. The pitch of the third varies between flat and natural. This notation is based on the performance during the fourth verse of the hymn.

In his book *Spiritual Folk-songs of Early America*, George Pullen Jackson wrote, "At camp meetings it was not a question of inducing every one to sing, but of letting every one sing, of letting them sing songs which were so simple that they became not a hindrance to general participation but an irresistible temptation to join in" (7). For this reason, long hymns with many verses frequently were reduced to simple choruses, composed of very short phrases, sung to equally simple tunes. Most likely this particular chorus was inspired by the longer hymn "Where We'll Never Grow Old," by Joseph C. Moore.

G major (Beginning: F below middle C; Ending: C) ♩= *126* (Beginning: ♩= 72   Ending: ♩= 160)

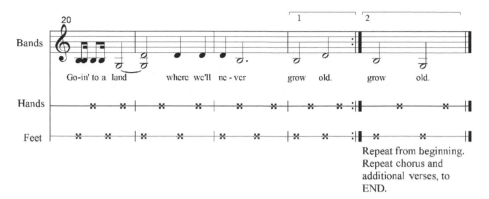

Repeat from beginning.
Repeat chorus and
additional verses, to
END.

VERSES:

2. Music, music in the air.
Goin' to a land where we'll never grow old.
I wish that music would come here.
Goin' to a land where we'll never grow old.

3. This old world is coming to an end.
What's gonna come of the wicked men?

4. Job, Job, where were you?
Old Job got in the kingdom too.

5. Ezekiel, Ezekiel saw the wheel.
Saw the wheel in the middle of the wheel.

6. What is it Jacob? What did you say?
Lord of a nation died today.

7. God told Hezekiah he had to die.
He turned to the wall and he began to cry.

Then you go back to the chorus, and just go over and over it. I guess any one of the men can tell them to start marching, then. All the captains will look at one another and nod their heads, or one of them will give the signal, "It's time to march."

The men will come around to our side of the bench and the women will go around to their side and sing a few minutes. The most that I have seen them march around the bench is two times. It all depends on how they feel. And then one of the men will give a nod and the men will march down one side aisle, and the women will march down the other. Sometimes the men will go ahead down the center aisle and will line up on each side of the aisle, and the women will come through the middle and go out the door.

Catherine Ennels and Buster Wilson lead a march at Union Chapel A.M.E. Church, outside of Cambridge, Maryland, expressing themselves as much with their hands as with their singing.

When the bands come out of the church and march outside, we form a ring. We're still singing the chorus and we're clapping just like they were inside the church. And then whoever wants to can get in the ring and put in a verse. And when they don't want to put in any more verses, they'll beckon somebody else to come in, or they'll catch somebody by the hand and pull him in to put in a verse.

And we'll just be motioning and clapping our hands. You march the way you want to march; everyone has their own motion. It's just something that's in you. And when someone is getting ready to put in a verse, I'll throw up my hands as a response, to let others know that we're putting in that verse. I have so many hand motions. That's just something that's in me. Gus Bivens looked like he had wings of an eagle. It's just his motion, his way of doing it.

It's a happy occasion. When the Spirit gets on them, they might do anything. That's their way of giving recognition to the Lord; that's their way of giving vent to their feelings.

When I see them shout like that, I always say they're in the Spirit, because you can't do it unless you're in the Spirit. And when the Spirit gets on you and you mean what you are doing, you don't get hurt. People run and get other peoples' glasses when they get happy; but if the Spirit is on you, you won't break your glasses. You do things in the Spirit you don't have any knowledge of later. You don't remember.

A nineteenth-century band leader remarked "at camp-meeting there must be a ring here, a ring there, a ring over yonder, or sinners will not get converted." The bands of today also conclude their prayer meetings by singing in an outdoor circle.

Years ago, when there were a lot of bands, then different nights throughout the week there would be either a prayer meeting or a class meeting. I know Mt. Zion's used to be on Friday night. (It was Mt. Zion then; the same church is now St. Luke.) And Wednesday night used to be Emmanuel Christian Church. I used to belong to St. John's, on Carrolton Avenue, between Lafayette and Lanvale Streets. We had a big band then: Mr. Hooper, Mr. Sam Henson, Sarah and Mary Henson, and Mr. Morris and Miss Suzie Neale, Miss Caroline and Miss Isabelle. And we used to go all through the week singing.

Back in those days, the women would work all day and didn't get paid much more than two dollars and carfare. Some of the men were stevedores or worked on the railroad. And the women would come home and fix dinner and wash up their kids and get them ready and take them to the service, to the prayer meeting or to the class meeting. My father was band captain before he went preaching. My mother used to get all seven of us ready and take us there—not every night, but many nights. The prayer meetings would start at 8:00 P.M. and go until 12:00 A.M., sometimes 12:30 or 1:00 A.M. And the children slept on the church benches until 12:00 or 12:30, and got up the next day and went to school. And we didn't miss a day of school.

Back then, there was nothing else to do *but* to go to church, and we would have a hallelujah time. That's why you go to the prayer meetings, you know, to forget

In this World War II–era photograph of the Singing and Praying Band of St. John's A.M.E. Church in Baltimore, Mary Allen stands in the second row, the second person from the right.

what you have been through that week, your troubles and trials. The fellowship is the main thing. You hear people testifying, how God brought them through, and you hear people pray for the sick and the afflicted. And you're praying that the Holy Spirit will come. You're saying, "Come Holy Spirit, come heavenly dove with all thy quickening power; come shed abroad the Savior's love in these cold hearts of ours," that we might have a *good* time.

It revives you. Someone will sing a hymn that will reflect on what you are going through and you all can feel the Spirit of the Lord moving in the church. The warm fire begins to burn, and you get a little warmer and warmer, and at the end you're on fire. Maybe I get happy and then somebody up front or the person behind me gets happy, and the Spirit runs from heart to heart and breast to breast.

It all makes sense; it does all make sense.

THREE

Samuel Jerry Colbert
(b. 1950)

There is no cross without a crown.

MY MOM DIED WHEN I WAS ABOUT SIX, so my grandmother raised my sister, Tere, and me from about age six to about twelve or thirteen, when my dad got remarried. My grandmother, Goldie Allen, held every position in Asbury Broadneck band from first captain to fourth captain, and she just went and went and went and she just dragged me and dragged me, and the band was all I knew. Sometimes if the Broadneck band had three camps to attend—which wasn't unheard of—they would leave home at 9:30 or 10:30 in the morning and get back home 10:00 or 11:00 at night. And we'd be in church *all day long*. Back then, people went to church to *stay* in church. In the fifties, there wasn't anything else for the old folks to do *but* go to church all day long.

From the time I got into the car, it was like a curse. They would start out, like on one particular Sunday, and go to Williamsburg, in Talbot County; that would be their first stop. Then they would go to Gum Swamp down towards Liner's Road, in western Dorchester County. And then we would come back up the road to Ivytown, in Talbot County. In the summertime those churches would be packed, and there was no air conditioning. With my white shirt and my little bow tie and this wool or gabardine blazer on, I used to roast to death.

Dressed in his Sunday best on a hot summer evening, a young boy claps along to the music under the tabernacle at Antioch A.M.E.'s August camp meeting in Frankford, Delaware.

And the little old ladies would come along and say, "How are you, Jerry?" They were all sweet; they were all sweet ladies. They would buy me ice cream and buy me pie.

But I just wanted to step on their toes. And I'd think, "Get away from me!"

That little Gum Swamp Church couldn't have been as big as this living room. By the time the Broadneck band lined up in front, there wouldn't be room for anybody else. They would give out a hymn, and by the time they got to the second verse, they'd be crying and they'd be caught up in the Holy Spirit. Those ladies would be jumping and shouting and carrying on.

Back then, because I was young and because I really wasn't interested, I never understood a word of the hymns. When I got to be about twelve years old I said to myself, "Boy, when I get big enough to baby-sit myself, I'm not ever going back to another camp meeting."

I hated it. I did, I just hated it.

They still had a mourners' bench, but I wasn't going to spend all that time down there. Those people just believed you've got to get your soul right. They believed that you just go up to the mourners' bench and tell God all about what a bad person you are, and how you want to change your life and give your life to Christ. And the amazing thing is that I never did understand when they thought that God had *really* come into your life and changed your life, because you'd hear stories, like, "I went to the mourners' bench for three nights in a row, and they prayed over me, and I prayed and prayed."

And I think, "Did you get tired on that third night and say, 'I can't, Lord. Here I am: take me, my knees are wearing out. It's been three nights now'?"

I wish I knew more about the mourners' bench, or who said that you had to come here and wrestle with God and go through all these emotions before the preacher would say, "You are now ready."

It isn't a thing between you and the preacher; it's a thing between you and God.

I was converted the more modern way. One day, at about age twelve or thirteen, I felt as though I needed a closer connection to God. And when they extended the invitation to Christian discipleship, I went up to the altar rail at Broadneck church and said, "I would like to become a member."

Though relegated to the past by the Methodist denominations, a mourners' bench is still a place of prayer for the Singing and Praying Bands.

They said, "Welcome."

And you went through a preparatory class, like, "This is what it means to be Methodist. This is what it means to be a church member." This is what it means to give your life to Christ: it's dedication; it is work; most of all it's being faithful to God and to your church.

I grew up in a family of ministers, and I just had this inner energy all of my life to be a leader and to share the word of God. To be a servant, really. I've never known it not to be a part of me, even from when I was a young kid and we used to play church. I would always say to myself, "I got to be the preacher, I got to be the preacher." From there it went on to be Methodist youth leadership. And from there into evangelizing. And from there into lay speaking, and now into preaching, and back to the Singing and Praying Band. I guess coming out of a religious background and people that really center their lives around faith, the band just becomes part of you.

The history of Asbury Broadneck goes back over one hundred and fifty years. You have to remember that we all went to Calvary Methodist, which was on State Circle in Annapolis. And the black people used to sit up in the balcony. And when they got tired of doing that, they all pulled out and built Asbury on West Street in Annapolis, which was our mother church.

And a man who had been a slave acquired some property from his former slave master over on Broadneck Peninsula, north of Annapolis. And at the time when he acquired his property, a group of band leaders or class leaders, whatever, got together and said, "Let's start a mission over here."

It wasn't on the present site, where Asbury Broadneck is now, but it was off of St. Margaret's Road, about a quarter of a mile away. And they had a little mission church. When the weather was bad, or on weekday evenings, they used to have church in schoolhouses or private homes.

When they were able to get the finances and land together, they built Asbury Broadneck Church. Very few members lived near Asbury Broadneck Church itself. They had members from Mulberry Hill, Brown's Woods, Skidmore, Arnold, and Severna Park. They thought this was a universal place to build a church because you had a community here, a community here, a community here, a community here.

And then as the community in Town Neck, to the north of Broadneck, grew, they built a small chapel in Severna Park and they pulled out of Broadneck. And in later years, the people in Arnold did the same thing; that is how Mount Calvary, in Arnold, came about.

Wednesday night and *after* preaching service on Sunday mornings—every Sunday—they would have prayer meeting. Within Broadneck, there were what we called class leaders. They were these older, seasoned members of the church. When you became a member of the church these people would take you under their wings. They were your spiritual leaders.

If I joined the church, for example, they might appoint Mr. Stepney, and say to me, "This is your spiritual leader." He would talk to you about the church, answer questions that you had, and be your guide. There were different class-meeting groups in the church, and every Sunday one of those groups had a class meeting and everybody came to support them.

The class leaders were pulled out of the Singing and Praying Bands, and class meeting was nothing more than a shorter version of camp meeting today. The band would open up the service with a hymn and a prayer. The congregation of the church would also get involved; they would line out a hymn by sitting in their pews. And then they'd have testimony and different people would get up and sing or whatever. And 90 percent of the time they ended with a band selection because the class leaders were band members and back then the band *was* the church.

Up until the early 1950s in Broadneck, the men would sit down on the left-hand side of the sanctuary, as you face the altar. The men always separated themselves from the women. The only time you saw a female on the left hand side of church was if she came to church late and there weren't any seats on the right side. I think the band pattern—the men always facing the ladies and the ladies always facing the

Carry Smith stands to testify at an outdoor class meeting on the campground of Union Wesley United Methodist Church, Clarksville, Delaware.

men—took structure from that, because back then the men were always the spiritual leaders of the church.

There were always more women than men in the band. If there were sixty or eighty band members, you only had twenty men. But the man has always been the leader of the band. There were female captains who were right beside that male captain, but it was the male captain that had the strong hold and gave directions. The female captain would give directions to the ladies.

That is what people did back then. There weren't a lot of choirs, and transportation wasn't that great, so you couldn't go from one church to another. So basically they stayed after church. And that was the life of the church, the Singing and Praying Band.

Broadneck always had one of the strongest Singing and Praying Bands. When I actually joined the band in '69 or '70, the Broadneck band still had a total of twenty-five to thirty members. We had two full rows of women and a full row of men.

Most churches had camp meeting for three weeks, and the band captain would arrange the whole thing. Although the integrated Methodist Conference of today doesn't know too much about the bands, the black conference in the past knew about the bands and supported them. They were the ones who spearheaded the revival services; they were the ones who spearheaded the fundraisers. That's who raised the money for the conference, up to five, six, seven, eight thousand dollars a year.

"Broadneck has always had one of the strongest bands." The sisters of Asbury Broadneck take center stage as the bands begin to sing at Magothy.

Marlon Hall and Clara Walters add up the offering at the camp meeting at Union Wesley United Methodist Church in Clarksville, Delaware.

Leteisha Hunt smiles impishly as she holds an offering plate during a camp meeting at Asbury Town Neck Church, Severna Park, Maryland.

2. The dying thief rejoiced to see that fountain in his day,
And there may I though vile as he wash all my sins away.

3. Dear dying lamb, thy precious blood shall never lose its power
Till all the ransomed church of God be saved to sin no more.

4. E'er since by faith I say the stream thy flowing wounds supply
Redeeming love has been my theme and shall be till I die.

5. Then in a nobler, sweeter song, I'll sing thy power to save
When this poor lisping, stammering tongue lies silent in the grave.

6. Oh weeping friend, don't weep for me while standing around my bed:
I know the way to Galilee, thank God I have no dread.

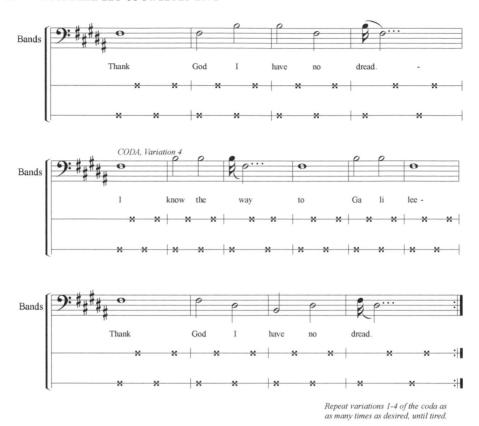

Repeat variations 1-4 of the coda as
as many times as desired, until tired.

There are some hymns you want to repeat every line two times. The particular tune that I use for "There is a fountain," we only sing the first line of the verse once, and then the second line we sing twice. The first line of this melody usually rises in pitch. The second line of the piece starts high, and then goes lower in pitch. You sing the second line twice. At the end of the first repetition of the second line, you raise the notes up to where you started it, so you know that it isn't finished. That means you are going to repeat the line again.

A lot of times I will choose the hymn I sing according to who is there. Louis Parker, captain of the band from Asbury in Annapolis, is a good one to help you to keep it in rhythm and tune. The older men are very good, but they don't always give it all that they can give. I have not sung "Vacation in Heaven" in over a year now. It's a very difficult hymn to sing and I need a lot of strong voices to pull that hymn. When I have all of the Broadneck women with me, I will sing it. But if I only have two or three, I'll just sing something more familiar, out of the hymn book.

I like to feel as though the total band is involved in the hymn before I will let myself go and be a part of the hymn. I will just let my eyes roam and if I see that two or three new people don't know the words and they are just timidly standing

Joseph Spicer of Christ United Methodist Church in Baltimore raises his hands over the mourners' bench to give out another verse of his signature hymn, "That Awful Day Will Surely Come."

Excerpts from "When I Take My Vacation in Heaven"
by Herbert Buffum (1879–1939), copyright 1925

Here so many are taking vacations
To the mountains the lakes and the sea;
Where they rest from their cares and their
      worries
What a wonderful time that must be.
But it seems not my lot to be like them
I must toil through the heat and the cold;
Seeking out the lost sheep on the mountains
Bringing wanderers back to the fold.

But someday I shall take my vacation
To that city John tells us about
With its foundation walls all so precious
Where from gladness of heart I shall shout!
Oh, no sights ever witnessed by mortals
Can compare with the glories up there.
I shall spend my vacation in heaven with Jesus
In the place He went up to prepare.

Now when most people take their vacation,
They return to their homes bye and bye.
But when I take my heavenly vacation
In my mansion of gold in the sky,
I will be with my Savior forever,
With him sit on his heavenly throne;
All the days will be one long vacation,
When my Savior takes me to his home.

When I take my vacation in Heaven,
What a wonderful time that will be!
Hearing concerts by the heavenly choirs,
And the face of my Savior I'll see.
Sitting down on the banks of the river,
'Neath the shade of the evergreen tree,
I shall rest from my burdens forever.
Won't you spend your vacation with me?

there, I will repeat the words to them again until I see they get it. And you can feel the communication, because they'll smile or they'll shake their heads and they get into it.

Raising the hymn up, picking up the speed just happens. That comes subconsciously. But if it's too slow, sometimes, it's like I say to myself, "This needs to be picked up, this needs to be picked up." You want it at the right speed but you don't want to get too fast. So you say to yourself, "We've got three more verses to do here, so we can't give it our all here right now."

The rhythm section, you have got to get that down. It's clap, and then you stomp, and clap, and then you stomp. The clapping actually is part of keeping the tune. It is like a drum. And you alternate feet; most of the time, it's just a left and a right and a left and a right, clapping in between. They start off very slow: left, right, left.

The foot patting is very soft in the beginning. Everything is kind of soft in the beginning. As we get into it, it gets louder. In the beginning the motion is kind of slow, and as you pick it its momentum, you just sway more, you get caught up in it, and you are rocking from side to side. And the more you get caught up in the spirit of it, the more the tempo picks up. The hymn becomes more a part of us. Maybe we will sway a bit more, or leap just a little bit higher. And if a person puts just a little extra into the motion or the singing, it is their testimony. It's their testimony; the emotional part comes out more in the hand gestures and the body motions.

Then there's the different hand signals. Basically, waving your hand in an upward motion means to keep it up. They just know that when my hand goes up, I want the

"Holding both your hands up means to stop singing and listen for the next verse." With the help of Mary Hunt, facing him, Rev. Jerry Colbert adds a verse to a give-out hymn at a band service on Taylors Island.

girls to help raise the hymn. Holding both your hands up means to stop singing and listen for the next verse. Waving both hands down means to stop the hymn.

At the end, you add a verse from a different hymn or a verse from the Bible, such as: "Oh weeping friend don't weep for me, while standing around my bed. / I know the way to Galilee, thank God I have no dread." That verse is a mixture of scripture and some old hymn. It's something that maybe inspired my great-great-great-grandfather and it's just something that we have hung onto down through the years. You add that when you're going to keep it forever—keep singing the last line—until you get tired of it.

When you get to that last line that we are going to sing over and over and over again until you get tired of it, you slow the tune down and in slowing it down, a lot of times you would change it a little bit, change the tune and the tempo. It becomes more of a chant. You are just singing two notes—the tonic and the third—and you are just swaying with it. It makes it easier for you; you don't have to think about anything.

Now, what I usually do is once I change the tune and slow it down, I'll sing it like that maybe three or four times. And then I will raise it: move up to something a little higher, you take it to the fifth, and then bring it back down to those two notes. And then when I repeat the cycle a second time, I'll keep it up on the fifth for two or three repetitions of the line. Then I drop it down again.

It gives you your final high. You are simply into it and you are putting your focus on your message. You don't have to scream it, and you don't have to shout it; you are chanting it. And by that time, you're into it, and hopefully the people in the congregation are into it.

I would say 99 percent of the people, when they get into it, you lose track of where you are, what you are doing, who's next to you and you are just caught up in it. You are just caught up in it until you feel a vibration, which we would say would be the Holy Spirit. It's just you and God in your own little world and you're looking forward to your eternal home, when things are all over with here. All the headaches, and children and bills and drugs and work and everything else . . .

Basically, God never promised that anything would be easy in life. And Jesus said that you must suffer as I suffered to enjoy the life that is to come. You're going to have some ups, you're going to have some downs. You are going to have some struggles. But I promise you eternal life. So that's where the saying "there is no cross without a crown" came in. When they talk about the crown, they talk about eternal life. But you can't earn that crown unless you are obedient to the word of God.

And you think of the words of Paul when he says, "The worst sinner that I was while I was on my way to persecute the church and it was Jesus who turned me around." And he said, "Just be a disciple and go into all the world and preach the

When you get caught up in the Holy Spirit, according to Jerry Colbert, "you lose track of where you are, what you are doing, who's next to you, and you are just caught up in it."

gospel." And discipleship is just kind of a *testimony* of what the Word is to you and what the Word has been to you. Basically, you have to work to be a Christian. You have to really *work* at it; it's an onward journey.

. . . The old folks used to call this chant at the end of a hymn "*working* the hymn." They get caught up in the familiar words, that ring home to them. It's like you personalize the words of the hymn. As people get caught up into it, their expressions of jubilance or their expressions of song come out in different ways. People have different ways of expressing their spirituality. It's their *testimony*. It's their testimony.

You are in total communion with God, you have this communication going back and forth, and it's just you and God. You are in your glory then. You've forgotten about the outside world; you forgot that it even exists. And you may hear somebody say, "Hallelujah!" or whatever. They're just carefree and happy now. It's just flowing, absolutely. It's just part of the Holy Spirit. It just happens.

In the older days, the band captains would just stop the singing. Basically, when you think it has run its course, or you have gotten your blessing, then you just bring it to a stop. I think now we get out of tune or we can see the ladies giving up on us, as if saying, "I've had enough; let's stop now."

A straight hymn is much simpler to raise. Basically, it is a chorus that is repeated over and over and over again. The leader and the band start out on their knees, and the leader would sing through the whole chorus, "All my appointed time, I'm gonna wait till my change comes . . ," on their knees. And usually when he repeats it a second time, we all stand up together and come forward. It's kind of quietly done. And again, basically, they have done that down through the years just to get themselves together, clear their minds, get focused on the next hymn.

You sing the chorus through three or four times, however many times, until you feel it. It starts slow, and it gets fast very quickly. The melody never changes. And then the leader throws in some verses, a Bible verse, or a verse from another hymn, like, "Job's wife, she asked him why, / Why don't you curse your God and die." And as soon as the others hear it, they all just jump on the same bandwagon and sing it along with him. They throw in the first line of one of these verses, and then sing the last line of the chorus; then the second line of the verse and then the last line of the chorus again. You repeat the verse two times, and then we go back to "All my appointed time." You can put in ten or fifteen verses; it depends upon how you are into the Spirit.

6. "All My Appointed Time"

A Straight Hymn

This transcription is based on the version of this hymn sung by the Eastern and Western Shore Singing and Praying Bands at Christ United Methodist Church in Baltimore on October 28, 1984. At the beginning of the hymn the tonic is A-flat below middle C, and the tempo is 80 quarter notes per minute. At the conclusion of the singing, the tonic has risen to B above middle C, and the tempo has increased to 200 quarter notes per minute. The pitch of the third varies between the minor and major third.

Longer songs on which this chorus seems to have been based have been recorded by numerous gospel artists under the titles "All My Appointed Time," "Blessed Be the Name," or "Job."

END: after final verse,
repeat chorus, and end
here.

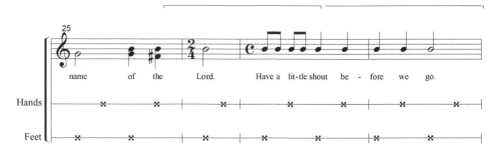

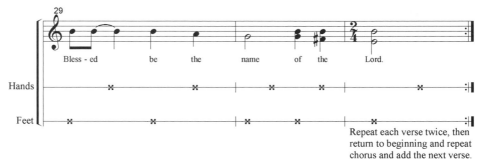

Repeat each verse twice, then
return to beginning and repeat
chorus and add the next verse.

VERSES:

2. I asked my Lord to fix me right.
Death might step in the house tonight.

3. Job's wife, she asked him why.
"Why don't you curse your God and die?"

4. Push out the lifeboat, let's go across.
Trust in the Lord, and you won't get lost.

5. My poor mother, she oftimes said,
"What ya gonna do, child, when I am dead?"

6. I feel my weakness every day.
Weakness tells me I must go away.

7. Push away, brethren, I don't care.
I'm gonna breathe my final prayer.

8. What you do if you had no Christ?
How you gonna get in paradise?

9. I feel my weakness every day.
Weakness tells me I must go away.

10. Ezekiel, Ezekiel, saw the wheel.
Saw the wheel in the middle of the wheel.

11. Job, Job, where were you?
Job got into the kingdom too.

12. I feel my weakness every day.
Weakness tells me I must go away.

13. Friends keep dropping out one by one.
I'm going too when my work's all done.

14. This campground I bid farewell.
This campground I bid farewell.

I was always told that in the beginning, a straight hymn was always to tell a story. So in this hymn you are talking about Job, so the verses would deal with Job. And then of course you are going to run out of verses about Job, so after that you add whatever new verse strikes one person as appropriate; it's a personal testimony. And then if it's the end of the meeting, the leader will just step back and two or three other people will take their turns, and they'll put in two or three verses. The leader will nod to someone, and also to one of the ladies, and she'll put in two or three verses and it goes along in that circle until you get tired.

In some straight hymns, the men would actually do the lead part, and the ladies would sing the refrain part, so that you wouldn't wear yourself out. Like in the hymn "Oh Sinner, Look to the Lord," Brother Stepney used to sing, "Oh sinner."

And the ladies would sing, "Oh, oh, sinner."

And he could rest and then he could come back again, "Oh sinner."

And they'd come back and sing, "look to the Lord."

That would give the ladies a breather, and then they would answer the men, and that would give the men a breather. The men would talk back to them; they would answer back to them.

7. "Oh Sinner, Look to the Lord"

A Straight Hymn

This notation is based on a performance of the Eastern and Western Shore Singing and Praying Bands recorded on July 7, 1991, at Jefferson United Methodist Church in Smithville, Maryland. Ike Hunt of Asbury Broadneck United Methodist Church led the hymn. At the beginning of the performance, the tonic was D above middle C and the piece was sung at 76 quarter notes per minute. The tonic rose steadily but unevenly during the hymn until at the end it was B above middle C, and the tempo was 176 quarter notes per minute.

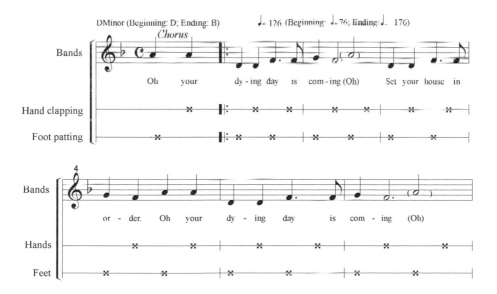

Repeat from beginning, add
new verses, return to chorus
to END.

VERSES:

2. And it's oh, Mona.
   Oh, Mona.
   Oh, Mona.
   Look to the Lord.

3. And it's oh, mother.
   Oh, mother.
   Oh, mother.
   Look to the Lord.

4. And it's oh, preacher.
    Oh, preacher.
    Oh, preacher.
    Look to the Lord.

5. And it's oh, Leda.
    Oh, Leda.
    Oh, Leda.
    Look to the Lord.

When the time has run out, or the last band has sung, we'll just go ahead and march around. Usually, we march around the mourners' bench or the chairs once. And they just march around the church. Once in a while, we'll come outside and sing in the yard. That concludes the service for the day.

But when I was a boy, I just hated the whole scene. I did, I hated it.

Yet, after I joined the church, and I joined the junior choir of the church, the band would start inviting the junior choir to sing behind the ministers who would preach at the camp meetings. I would travel with the choir. And I guess the rhythm of the band that was embedded in me from those six years with my grandmother just came to life again. It came to life.

Back when the Singing and Praying Bands started, they were an evangelizing tool for the minister. They'd pray for a particular soul to come to Christ. They'd pray for certain things to either happen or not happen within the community, in the church, in the world. People looked forward to camp meeting because relatives that had moved away were certain to come home during camp-meeting time. And then other people would come just to pray for their wayward children. And even though for a lot of young people it was a time to play and run around and buy candy and soda, the older folks had another theory in mind. They would be hoping that some of the young people would run into church during one of those services and give their lives to Christ.

Unfortunately in this twenty-first century that we live in, the Singing and Praying Band is more of a tradition than an evangelizing tool. And the younger people that are in the band today, it's simply because when they were growing up, they were attached to someone who was part of it. Grandmother, grandfather, uncle, it's just someone that they attached themselves to, and it just became part of you. It's just part of you; it's a family thing. It's a tradition. It becomes part of you and you don't completely let it go.

There are times now when I do get frustrated with the bands. I guess on any given day nobody is 100 percent. But it's those times when nobody wants to sing—or we sing and then before I can get anything out of it, they may just stop and go home—that I think, "Why did you even bother to come? Let's not lose track of tradition here. The tradition still says that the purpose of the Singing and Praying Bands is to bring sinners to Christ. So if you are not going to pray, you are not going to sing, why did you even bother to come out?"

And I often think, what were people like my grandmother made out of, to go to church all day long? And then bright and early Monday, they're up again going back to work. And now, it's like, "We can't sing after four o'clock service, sing after 8:00 P.M. That is too late, we've got to get to work tomorrow."

The old folks are still an inspiration; it's the young folks who want to go home. I think the young folks like the tradition, but I think they lose some portions of it, of the purpose. The only way they'll get that back, we get that back, is through training, and teaching and, as you would say, tarrying. But no, I don't get tired of the band. There are moments of frustration.

A year or so ago, a group within the United Methodist Church called the Black Methodists for Church Renewal had their conference in Baltimore. And they invited the bands to attend. We were dressed in our uniforms and we concluded the service just like usual, because we were in a church.

They were so impressed. And they said, "We used to have camp meeting, but our camp meetings were more like revival. This is so unique. This is so unique."

Rev. Lewis Watson offers up a fiery sermon to bring the church to life at the camp meeting at Mt. Zion United Methodist in Magothy, Maryland.

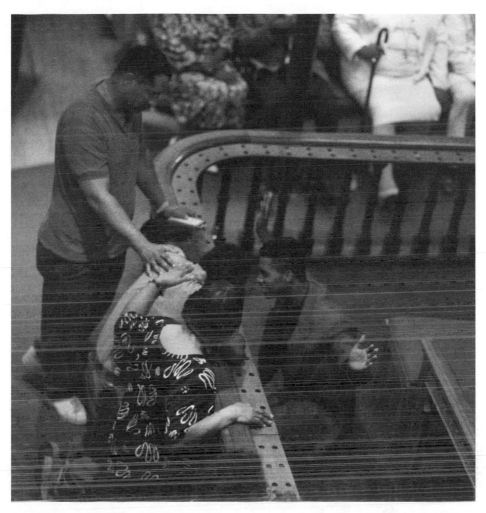

A new convert stumbles into church during a camp meeting, kneels and prays at the altar rail, and is welcomed by three church members.

FOUR

Gertrude Stanley
(b. 1926)

There must be a wheel in the middle of the wheel.

I COME FROM HARRISVILLE; that's my roots. Taylors Island is not my home, but my husband's home was down here. I didn't join the band until I came to Taylors Island. I started working with the camp, about ever since I moved down here in 1948.

This is Dorchester County. If you are coming from Cambridge, you go south on Route 50 until you get out of Cambridge. And you would make a right turn at the light to come to Taylors Island. The road is Route 16.

And the next community that you get to would be Christ Rock. We call it Christ Rock. And you come on through Christ Rock and the next village you get to would be the village of Church Creek, about ten miles. And you go on through Church Creek, and you would see a sign that says, "You are ten miles from Taylors Island."

After you come through Church Creek, then its Woolford (in order to get to Harrisville, the colored community, you have to turn off to your left at Woolford, and go down Harrisville Road). And the next community that you get to would be Madison. Most black people in Madison are down what they used to call White Marsh Road.

And after that, you would see nothing but a few houses and a long stretch of woods. Its Christ Rock, then Church Creek, then Harrisville, and after Harrisville would be Madison, after Madison it would be Taylors Island. You bypass Smithville. You have to turn off Route 16 to get to the colored section of Smithville.

Each community back in those days had a full community of people. They were all related, yes, indeed. Some of the men from Smithville married women and went to Harrisville. And some of the women from Harrisville married people from Smithville. That's how they would go. As far back as I can remember, they would leave one community and go to another. But they were still people that worked together.

Rock is a Methodist church, Harrisville is, Madison was, but they don't have a church there anymore. And then Smithville and Taylors Island church are Methodist churches. They were the Taylors Island charge.

I worked in a sewing factory in Cambridge for over nineteen years. And then they went out of business. And from there I went to doing seasonal work. In the sum mertime, I worked in the canning factory. Most of the people were from around this area. I used to go from here over to Sherman Wilson's (Sherman and Florence were

A surprised Gertrude Stanley watches the camera as she fries oysters for the fellowship dinner at a Taylors Island camp.

from Smithville; I married Sherman's wife's brother, Albert) and get on his bus and go to work at Friendship Cannery in Federalsburg in Caroline County.

When I first started going there, I worked on the belt, cleaning tomatoes, picking out green tomatoes and the leaves and stems. They would scald them and take the skins off. Then I went back into the warehouse putting the cans on the line that would run down to the packing tables. And the ladies on the packing table would push the tomatoes down and they'd go right straight down the line. There was always somebody on the line that would put the salt balls in—keep the machine full so the balls would drop in each can of tomatoes. Then they would go to the capper, and then keep right on to the cooker. They would cook the tomatoes.

They didn't pay too much; minimum wage, I am sure that is what it was.

I loved to shuck oysters, but it was hard. Where we shucked, the owner had people pulling a bushel basket of oysters on a cart. And they would take them and plunk them up on your table. The majority of the tables were to the side, against the wall. But some of the tables were in the middle of the floor and you had somebody on each side of it, facing each other. There would be about eight people on each table, four on each side.

If you start around September or October, the oysters are hard to open. I used to hit mine with a piece of iron, because they will tear your hand up. You take a knife and open the mouth to shuck them, and run your knife in and cut the heart from the shell. Then you turn it over and take it out and put it in your bucket.

When you got the bucket full, you carried it back to the man who skimmed oysters. Whites didn't shuck oysters but they would work in the skimmer room. They called it weighing them up. You carry your oysters up to this hole and pour them out over a tray that has holes in it, and the juice would run out. And then you would have a dry gallon of oysters. He would put them on the scale and weigh them.

Then, they would put them in this container in some kind of solution, a big machine in the middle of the floor that would "blow" them. They called it blowing the oysters. And it would wash them, get the grit and stuff out of them. And when they came out, they would be really white and clean. Then there was a belt or a line, and the oysters would run down into those little round pint or half-pint cans. Then they would put caps on them, and box them up. That's how they would do it.

Anything I did, I liked. I just knew that was the way I had to make my living. Then, you'd be working with people that kept something going all the time. If somebody wanted to sing, and if somebody felt like they wanted to join in, they'd join in. If they didn't, they just kept on laughing and talking and telling jokes. They loved those jokes better than anything else.

They would tell different things that would make you laugh. Some of them were fibs—little lies. They would tell of their experiences and they would tease each other. They didn't put each other down or try to make each other look small; they just found something to laugh about. One man who worked on our table—Nelson Nutter from Nanticoke—was so much fun that we are talking about him now, after he's dead.

The spirit of "help" lives on in the oyster-shucking houses, as a younger man takes time out to shovel a load of oysters onto the table for the benefit of the older workers.

Three buckets of shucked oysters represent a significant amount of income to Catherine Ennels of Cambridge, Maryland, who continued to work in her senior years.

I was twenty-two when I got married; I was twenty-two when I got married to Albert Stanley. His home was down here on Taylors Island. I started working with the camp meeting about ever since I moved here. When I first came, they didn't have conveniences at the church. They used to haul water on a cart or wagon, and it would sit up there on the church ground. There would be a tent that they used to call a pavilion, and they used to have preaching and band singing outside on sawdust and straw because it would be too hot in the church. But nobody camped on the campground.

Now, our camp starts on the first Sunday in August. But it used to always start on the last Sunday in July. And the first Sunday in August was the last Sunday. And that's when the people came from the Western Shore and stayed all night long. And early that Monday morning, they would start class services just like they do down in Magothy on Monday morning. And then they would sing and pray for a while. And I think they didn't cut that service out until around twelve noon.

The women of the bands always did the cooking. I guess they would start getting it ready about Saturday for that Sunday morning. They would go up there early, start cooking the food. They used to cook on wood stoves.

They always did have chicken, ham, the old-time country hams. People cured the ham themselves, I guess. They used to kill chickens then. *Good Lord, have mercy!*

With its steeple cross leaning and roof sections seeming to sag, Lane Church embodies the beleaguered dignity common to many economically troubled Eastern Shore churches where the Singing and Praying Bands once thrived.

People used to raise chickens then, and they would buy the chickens from somebody and kill them and dress them. And people raised potatoes and string beans in their gardens. They would make pies, yes, indeed, sweet potato pies. And they might have had white potato pies, too, because they liked that kind of thing. Probably a dinner might have cost two dollars.

They would be cooking all day long. Now the camp is over about 5:00 P.M. Sunday. Back then it lasted longer. That Monday morning, the same people who toiled all day long and all night long cooked breakfast. They were doing it for the church.

Back then, I didn't do much cooking. I might do the dishes or set the tables up or something. You just start helping. When I started cooking, we weren't picking any chickens; we were getting that stuff from the store.

I got converted down to Harrisville, when I was real young, about fourteen or fifteen. A gang of us were going together to Harrisville church because our parents told us to go. We were just going there for fun then. But after that foolishness gets out of you, and the Holy Spirit got on you and you got converted or whatever you mind to call it—some people say, "I got saved"—then you know what it was all about, and you put away that foolish stuff.

In the kitchen of the fellowship hall at Lane Church on Taylors Island, the dedicated women of the band clean up after a long, hot afternoon of cooking for those who attended their camp meeting.

You had to be a preparatory member for about five or six months. And then they would read you into the church and enlighten you on some of the things that you were expected to do.

As you first start out, you are bashful. One time, my aunt asked me to give the welcome address or something at the church. And I didn't want to do it. I didn't know what to do. And so I said to myself, "I know what to do. I'll be late going to church, so the program will be well on its way when I get there."

And that is what I did. I said to myself, "Lord, I *know* she ain't going to call on me now."

But it didn't help, because she called on me anyway. I couldn't get away from it.

Naturally, you grow in grace. You grow. You have to work on it. But no, indeed, I didn't join the band until I came down to Taylors Island. And it was a long period of time before they ever called on me to pray.

No longer able to muster the physical energy to participate in a band service, nonagenarian Ralph Opher of Cambridge, Maryland, offers words of blessing to those who keep on keeping on.

When you pray to him, you need him to come into your life. You learn to pray by growing and listening to other people pray and listening to sermons being preached. Sometimes it comes from what you have read in the Bible. I guess when you go to kneel down, the word of the Lord just comes to you. You don't plan it; you can't plan it. It's just something that comes to you.

[Gertrude Stanley offered the following prayer during a service of the Eastern Shore Singing and Praying Bands during a camp meeting at St. Paul's United Methodist Church, Harrisville, Maryland, on August 17, 1986.]

"When that illustrious day shall rise
And all thy armies shine,
In robes of victory through the skies
The glory shall be thine."

Lord, we've come this afternoon
        with no merits of our own
                no goodness to be claimed.
    We've come as empty pitchers
        to the well
        to be fulfilled.

We've come
    Just to say, "Thank you
        For being God
        And letting us be thy believing children."
We have come, almighty God
    Just to say,
        "Try us, oh God,
        and search the ground
            Of every sinful heart;
        Whatever sin in us is found
            Oh, get it all to part.

"And when to the right
    or to the left we stray,
    Oh Lord, leave us not comfortless,
        But guide our feet
            Into the way
                Of everlasting peace."

I know, this afternoon
    That you are the same God
        Heard my prayer a long time ago,
        And told me every knee must bow,
            Every tongue
                Must confess
        Thou art God
        Besides thee there is no other.

You are the lily of the valley;
You are the bright and the morning star;
You are the root
    and the branch of David.

You are the same God
    That heard Daniel
        When he prayed in the lion's den;
    Heard Rachael
        When she prayed in the cliffs of the mountain;
    You heard the three Hebrew boys
        When they prayed in the fiery furnace.

You are the same God
    That heard me one day
        When I was lying
        Next door to hell.
    You stooped just a little while,
        Snatched my soul from eternal burning,
        Told me to go in peace,
            Sin no more.

But, oh Lord,
    Since that day—
I said, since that day—
I have sinned against you,
        High head and outstretched arms.

But this afternoon, Lord,
    I'm asking you to forgive me
        For my many sins,
    And wash me
        in your precious blood
            takes all my sins away.

You know, Lord, I'm a motherless child;
        I'm a fatherless child
            A long way from home.
        But I've heard of a city called heaven.
            I'm just striving to make it my home.

I want you to bless the sick;
I want you to bless the afflicted.
        Bless the poor,
            And the needy.

We need you, my Lord,
        Can't get along without you.
            My arms are too short,
            And my faith grows weak.

Increase my faith;
Confirm my hope;
Perfect me in love.

And when I've gone the last mile of the way,
I'm gonna rest at the close of the day.
I know there are joys that await me
When I've gone the last mile of the way.

I want you to bless the band sisters and brothers.
We are growing
Old in age.
Footsteps are being measured to the tomb.

I want you to build us up
Where we are torn down;
Strengthen us when we are weak.
For we need you,
Every hour I need you.
Bless me
Right now
My savior
I have come to thee.

This is where
I first saw the light
And the burdens of my heart
Was rolled away.

But it was since that day, Lord—
You know me,
You made me—
Increase my faith;
Confirm my hope;
Perfect me in love.

You say not for a long prayer,
So many fine words,
But the race was to him or her
That endureth to the end.
The very same shall be saved,
When I've gone the last mile of the way.

When my face
Has become like a looking glass,
I want you to own me
In judgment.
I want you to crown me
With everlasting salvation,
Where my name shall have all the praise.

I'll be able to praise thee
    in a better world than this.

I'll be able to walk through the streets of the city
    With my loved ones.
        Gone on before.
I'm going to sit down by the banks of the river;
I'm going to rest
    Forever more.

These and all other blessings we ask in your name,
        For your sake.
    My soul says, "Amen."

Lord, you know me
    Because you made me.
    He said if you make man,
        He'll sin
. . . come back to the father.

I ask you to forgive me of my many sins,
    Wash me in your precious blood
        Takes all my sins away.

I guess when you go to kneel down, the words of a hymn, like "Am I a Soldier of the Cross," are on your mind, and these are the words that come to you:

When that illustrious day shall rise
And all thy armies shine,
In robes of victory through the skies
The glory shall be thine.

I guess you could say it gives you a closeness to God or a calmness. It helps you get yourself together, to get ready to move on.
    For example, my father used to *say* this piece a lot:

I think when I hear that sweet story of old
When Jesus was here among men,
He called little children like lambs to the fold,
I should have loved to have been with him then.

I wish that his hands had been placed on my head,
And his arms had been thrown around me;
That I might have seen his kind look when he said,
"Let the little ones come unto me."

Down to his footstool in prayer we will go,
And ask for a share of his love;
If we just earnestly seek him below,
We shall see and hear him above.

In that beautiful place he has gone to prepare,
For all who are washed and forgiven;
Where many dear children shall gather there,
For such is the kingdom of heaven.

He would sometimes get up and start off his testimony with that. I had it in a hymn book one time, but I don't know what hymn book that was. He might not have said it all, but as the years went by, I learned it from hearing it from different people.

Lord we've come this afternoon
        with no merits of our own
            no goodness to be claimed.
    We've come as empty pitchers
        to the well
        to be fulfilled.

"Empty pitcher" means you are empty. One woman was saying last Sunday, "Fill my cup, Lord. Fill it up!" because it is empty and you need to go back to him to be revived.

"To the well to be fulfilled" is just a saying. You are not purely empty, but you're seeking fulfillment. *We* are pitchers, and we come before the fountain, the full fountain, come before God, to be revived. You want his Holy Spirit to fill you.

When some people are praying, I will say, "Amen." When you say "Amen" you're saying, "That is so; it's well done." Maybe they have said something that you could apply to your life. You feel like they are on the mark, and then you respond.

That's what the preacher said Sunday, "When I preach, I'd like you to talk back to me." He wanted you either to say "Amen," or "Ouch!"

You feel your way along, it doesn't come all at once. People call out, "Take your time." Sometimes that takes your thoughts away. But then, sometimes it encourages you. It probably will help you some.

We have come almighty God
    Just to say
        "Try us, oh God,
        and search the ground
            Of every sinful heart;
        Whatever sin in us is found
            Oh, get it all to part."

That's from "Try us, oh God, and search the ground," one of those old hymns they don't even put in the hymn book anymore. Viola Opher, Ralph Opher's wife, used to give that out in the band.

> I know, this afternoon
>   That you are the same God
>   Heard my prayer a long time ago,
>   And told me every knee must bow,
>   Every tongue
>   Must confess
>   Thou art God
>   Besides thee there is no other.

"Every knee must bow and every tongue must confess," that's in the Bible too [Phil. 2:10–11]. They sing that as a straight hymn too: "Every knee must bow, every tongue must confess, every knee must bow one day."

> You are the lily of the valley;
> You are the bright and the morning star;
> You are the root
>   and the branch of David.

You've got to give God some praise for what he's brought you through and how he's given you health and strength. That's the way I feel.

"The bright and the morning star," that's in the Bible. Some of them might have heard it over the years, about God being the lily of the valley [Song of Sol. 2:1] and the bright and the morning star [Rev. 22:16], but some might have read it in the Bible. "The root and the branch of David"—I know that's in there [Isa. 11:1; Rev. 22:16]. And they've got a hymn of that too, "I am that I am":

> I heard Jesus say
> I am the way [John 14:6];
> I am the root and the branch of David [Rev. 22:16];
> I am that I am [Exod. 3:14].

They call that a fly-away hymn. A fly away hymn is the same as a straight hymn. To tell you the truth, I heard that in a group singing; the Young family—they're from down on the other side of somewhere—used to sing that as a group piece. I did hear Gus Bivens say that in a prayer, "You are the root and the branch of David; you are the chief cornerstone, laid back in Zion," and all that. Sometimes I can't tell you where I found it, but I do know I have read that in the Bible.

8. "I Heard Jesus Say"

A Straight Hymn

The musical notation below is based on a version of this traditional song that Benjamin Beckett, of Antioch African Methodist Episcopal Church in Frankford, Delaware, sang as part of his testimony during an experience service at a camp meeting at Lane United Methodist Church, Taylors Island, Maryland, on August 1, 1999. The pitch of B varies between B-flat and B-natural. The pitch of F varies between F-flat and F-sharp.

You are the same God
> That heard Daniel
>> When he prayed in the lion's den;
> Heard Rachel
>> When she prayed in the cliffs of the mountain;
> You heard the three Hebrew boys
>> When they prayed in the fiery furnace.

You are the same God
> That heard me one day
>> When I was lying
>> Next door to hell.

You *know* all of *those* stories are in the Bible. We are just remembering what he did for those other people, like Rachel or Daniel. And it seems like it just touches your heart remembering what he was to those people of old. Maybe it's on your mind what he has done for them, and how they came through, and how he's still there. He's still the same today as he was yesterday.

And I'll tell you the truth: sometimes you start saying a lot of things, and then you start reading in the Bible and you run across it and you say, "Oh, that's where that comes from, it's right here."

A stalwart presence at every camp meeting for years, Joseph Spicer expresses his all-encompassing joy with outstretched arms at St. Paul's Church in Harrisville, Maryland.

There's a piece, a hymn of thanksgiving for what he has done, and I read *it* in the Bible:

> Jesus fed me
> When I was hungry,
> Give me a little drink when I was dry,
> Yes, he clothed me when I was naked.
> Bless his name; bless his name. [Matt. 25:35–36]

You thank him what he has done for you, just praise him anyway you can. You know that you are serving a God that is real. Sometimes right here around in this house, if I get to reading the Bible, some of the verses I read compare with my life and I say, "This is *good!*" and I just get up rejoicing.

9. "Jesus Fed Me When I Was Hungry"

A Straight Hymn

The notation below is based on a version of this song performed by the Eastern Shore Singing and Praying Band at Friendship United Methodist Church outside of Millsboro, Delaware, in October 1983, led by Ralph Opher of Cambridge, Maryland. The performance began at a tempo of 112 quarter notes per minute, with A below middle C as the tonic note. The pitch and tempo rose steadily throughout the performance, till peaking at 180 quarter notes per minute, with D above middle C as the tonic. The pitch of the third oscillates between minor and major. The text, drawn from Matthew 25:34–40, represents a familiar motif in black spirituals.

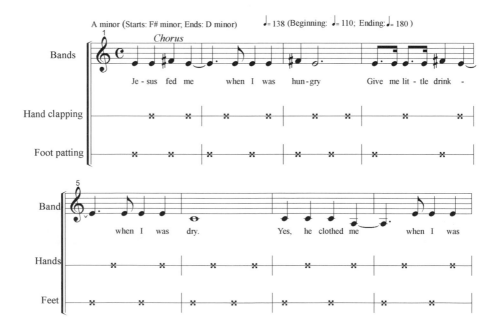

VERSES:

2. Give me the witness and he told me to go.
Give me the trumpet and he told me to blow.

3. Job, Job, where were you?
Old Job got into the kingdom too.

4. He hung on the cross till the sun went down.
The dead saints got up and walked around.

The burdens have fallen away. They are not gone away, because everyday you encounter something different in your life. Always.

> But this afternoon, Lord,
> I'm asking you to forgive me
> For my many sins,
> And wash me
> in your precious blood
> takes all my sins away.

A woman preached about this the other day: the things that already passed, just let them be. You are asking him to forgive your sins and dump them in the sea of forgetfulness—"don't remember them against me any more!"

I think the chorus, "Wash me in your precious blood takes my sins away," is from the hymn "There Is a Fountain Filled with Blood."

> You know, Lord, I'm a motherless child;
> I'm a fatherless child
> A long way from home.
> But I've heard of a city called heaven.
> I'm just striving to make it my home.

The second part—"I've heard of a city called heaven"—that's a hymn, "I am a poor pilgrim of sorrow." Roosevelt Cornish used to give that out. He was from Taylors Island but lived over in Smithville. He married a woman named Maggie Opher from Smithville.

I guess you are just thanking God for your mother, and how she taught you what you are going to face in this world.

My mother passed in June 1956. I told you I did a lot of seasonal work. I was picking beans; I was picking beans that day. We were going up to Hurlock or Williamsburg, in eastern Dorchester County, on the bus. And we came back to Church Creek—they always stopped by Church Creek because there used to be two or three stores there, and they liked to buy popsicles and ice cream.

And when we got to Church Creek, there was a man from Madison who came to the bus and said, "Miss Gertrude, your mother got burnt up."

I said, "What?"

He said, "Your mother got burnt up. They done carried her to the hospital."

And I said, "For the Lord's sake."

My mother's name was Sarah, but they called her Sally, Sally Harris. She lived in Woolford. She had washed that day.

We were using wood stoves. And she was getting ready to make a fire to cook her supper. The oil can was sitting right by the door, and the sun had been shining on it, on the oil can. And she had been washing, and already had had a fire in the stove. That's how she had to heat the water back in those days. And I guess by washing and hanging clothes, the fire had gone out. She was going to start this fire all over and cook her supper. When she poured this coal oil in there, that flame just "psssh . . ." in her face and on her hands. It burned her fingers right off her hand.

When she hollered, she swallowed the flame. And that's what burnt her insides up.

And Minnie Lee—she's a friend—was going down to see some of her friends in Harrisville. And she saw her, because she had run outdoors into the yard. She didn't have anything to roll in and that fire had just caught on to her clothes and everything.

My father had gone to the store, and Minnie Lee went back and picked him up.

That bus couldn't leave Church Creek fast enough for me. I started to get off the bus and walk, but how was I going to walk from there to Taylors Island? Finally the others came out from the different stores, and I came home and we got ready and went back up to the hospital.

She never did regain consciousness. My father had a time. My mother was a going woman; my father was a home-staying man. He was just a man who depended on her.

Overcome with the Spirit, Joseph Spicer takes a moment to wipe away his tears.

It was hard, but I tried not to let it get me down. You can be bogged down in it, but I was never like that. I was for that day, or that week, but I didn't dwell there.

And I say, I know that I am serving a God that is able. I know we are all born to die, and I know that it was written in the book that we are born to leave this world. It didn't say *how* we were going to leave here. But I try to lean on his promise that he would never leave you and that he would never forsake you. And I know God is real and I know just what he can do. And that's what carried me through. That's why I say your prayers come through.

> I want you to bless the band brothers and sisters,
> We are growing
> Old in age.
> Footsteps are being measured to the tomb.

> I want you to build us up
> Where we are torn down;
> Strengthen us when we are weak.

You are not just praying for yourself only, or your family. You are supposed to pray for others. Sometimes you have hills that are really high and you can't climb them. And your valleys are so low you want him to fill them up. So you tell him what you want: "Knock down our high hills; build up the low valleys."

> For we need you,
> Every hour I need you.
> Bless me
> Right now
> My Savior
> I have come to thee.

An invocation *is* a prayer: "Be present right now! Come closer!" Most everybody says, "I need you." You know you need him ever hour, just like that piece they sing, "I need thee, every hour I need thee."

Sometimes in church, when they get to singing "I need thee every hour, most gracious Lord, come quickly and abide," you just listen and apply the words to your life. *There's just something about that hymn* makes you feel the presence of the Lord. This might be one week that you really need God to come to your rescue. Or you just needed his presence.

(I tell you what, I loved to hear my husband sing, sing in the band, or just ordinary singing Sunday morning in the church. I loved the voice he had. *There was just something about his voice.* There's a hymn that he used to sing, "There's something about that name." But *there was something about his voice* that carried me through. His sister and his other two brothers could sing, but to me his voice was the sweetest. You hear some people who sing because they can sing. But he sang with spirit. To me, that's what it was about his voice. He sang with spirit. When you sing with the Spirit, that's what touches me.)

Sometimes, a praying person can just be praising the Lord and then it just touches you and makes you want to praise him too. They are saying what's on their mind and what's in their hearts. And after they get down a little further in their prayer, you know the Holy Spirit has got hold of them because they have changed and their voices have changed, and you know that God is with them. It makes you feel like you know what they are talking about and what they are going through, and the Spirit is flowing from heart to heart and breast to breast.

It makes you feel like there must be a wheel in the middle of the wheel. We used to sing that piece in church back in those days: "Ezekiel, Ezekiel saw the wheel, way in the middle of the air; the big wheel runs by faith and the little wheel runs by the grace of God—A wheel in the middle of the wheel." They used to sing that piece. But it's in the Bible about the wheel [Ezek. 1:15–21].

That's the feeling that you have when the Holy Spirit is going around to everybody. It seems like the Spirit that's within them just flowed from them to you, making you feel like you want to praise him too. Your inner self is connected with his Spirit, and you just feel like you are free. The Spirit of God makes everybody feel like that. Everybody.

Rocking first to one side and then to the other, (front to back) Joe Louis Parker, Shawn Copeland, Alfred Green, and Jerry Colbert lead a line of men out of St. Paul's Church in Harrisville.

You can see it; you can feel it, when it's going along good, and everybody is touching on one thing and the Spirit is with everybody. It runs around in that circle. You *know* what's in the middle of it. It's got to be God.

Back in time, the Singing and Praying Bands would get in a circle and sing. There used to be a band from Butlertown, and when they used to come around here, they used to sing in a circle, outside. But now the bands face each other, men and women. They don't really get in the circle until the end. They march out of church, and then you might see them get in a circle, and somebody will get in that circle to put a verse in the fly-away hymn.

We start our camp meetings in June. We go around to all those churches until December. And they all return the visit. That creates that wheel again; that's the wheel alright.

> This is where
> I first saw the light
>   And the burdens of my heart
>   Was rolled away.

I was at St. Paul's Church in Harrisville, at a camp meeting when I prayed this prayer.

Harrisville is where I first joined the church. I wanted to get acquainted with this God that my mother and my father and my aunt were talking about. They were having this revival and I remember the preacher asked, "Does anybody want to confess Jesus Christ as their savior? Well, come down to the altar."

You know how the older people would go down to the altar with you? I remember my aunt would say, "Call on the name of the Lord Jesus Christ, and he will save you."

And I just kept doing that. Sometimes if you stay down there too long, they would take you up and say, "Come back another night; maybe you can get what you are seeking for."

When we were converted, we were shouting, rejoicing, singing, just praising him any way you could. You knew it was real.

> But it was since that day, Lord—
>   You know me,
>   You made me—
>   Increase my faith;
>   Confirm my hope;
>   Perfect me in love.
>
> You say not for a long prayer,
>   So many fine words,
> But the race was to be to him or her
>   That endurest to the end.
> The very same shall be saved,
>   When I've gone the last mile of the way.

The prayer meeting completed inside Harrisville's church, Katherine Marine motions the marchers on toward the fellowship hall.

The sisters leading the way, the entire Singing and Praying group marches down the ramp toward the fellowship hall nearby.

"You know me, you made me"; you don't have to tell every Tom, Dick, and Harry the situations that you go through because they can't solve it. All they can do is talk about it.

Like if you have some children and you can't tell them anything—you know how you can't tell children anything sometimes? Then you say, "I'm leaving it in the hands of the Lord." So you just take it to the altar and say, "Lord, you know my child. You know his circumstances and you know what he is going through. But I know that you are a God that solves problems. I'm going to leave it in your hands."

"Not for a long prayer" means you don't have to say a whole lot of fine words because some people just get down there and say a whole lot of repetitions. You don't have to say a long prayer and you don't have to say a lot of fancy words. No, no, no.

> When my face
> > Has become like a looking glass,
> > I want you to own me
> > > In judgment.
> I want you to crown me
> > With everlasting salvation,
> > > Where my name shall have all the praise.
> I'll be able to praise thee
> > in a better world than this.
>
> I'll be able to walk through the streets of the city
> > With my loved ones.
> > > Gone on before.
> I'm going to sit down by the banks of the river;
> I'm going to rest
> > Forever more.

"When my face has become like a looking glass": when you have a funeral, people come and look down on you. That is the way I take it to be. Yes, you *are* going to be crowned when you get there, you know.

And "I'm going to walk through the streets of the city with my loved ones gone on before": that's a fly-away hymn. Gus Bivens gave that out.

> These and all other blessings we ask in your name,
> > For your sake
> > My soul says, "Amen."
>
> Lord, you know me
> > Because you made me.
> > He said if you make man,
> > > He'll sin.
> > Come back to the father.
>
> I ask you to forgive me of my many sins,
> > Wash me in your precious blood
> > > That takes my sins away.

The last of the Singing and Praying Bands marches away toward Harrisville's fellowship hall, where they will sing for those assembled there.

Relaxing after a long day in the kitchen of Taylors Island's church, Julia Cornish and Betty Irving rest behind the fellowship hall.

Some people just say "Amen", some people say "this is your servant's prayer, my soul says 'Amen.'"

Sometimes they just have some more they want to say. That's why they keep going. Something else comes in your mind and you just have to tell it.

Albert and I were married thirty-five years before he died. And if he had been living today, we'd be married over fifty years. Sure I miss Albert at times. But I don't get lonesome, because I can think of good times, hard times, bad times. But through it all, we made it. We made it. We made it.

Of course, I never really had a whole lot of personal problems, but sometimes, even in a community of people, you are just right here alone. Not lonesome, but you could have somebody to talk to every now and then. Then if you don't have that person, you can talk to God. And he comes in and he just fills you up. You feel good, sometimes right here in this house. He comes into your life and the things that you were depressed about or the things that you had problems with pass by, and you don't know how they passed or when they passed.

Some people don't have a peace of mind, and the least little thing upsets them. But I have a peace of mind, because I know where to go to get a peace of mind. And I know that he is a God that will answer your prayer and a God that will come to your rescue.

Rev. Edward Johnson
(1905–91)

Together let us sweetly live.

I TELL YOU, IF THE OLD FOLKS didn't know the Lord in those times, I don't know how they would have fared, because they couldn't make any money. And some of them had six or seven or eight in the family. It was tight, but they made it.

My parents didn't own any land; they worked for white folks, mostly. Then, after about 1915, they commenced to own some land. In those days land was really cheap. You could buy an acre of land for about twenty dollars, but it was hard to get that twenty dollars to buy the land. You worked all day long for only fifty cents. Of course, you could take that fifty cents and you could do right well with it, like get sugar and supplies like that. They grew most of their other food, like cabbage and potatoes, and they raised chickens and hogs.

In those times, people were more loving than they are now. Anybody who had children at that time and their children went to somebody else's house, when it came time that those people thought that the children ought to be home, they would tell you, "Look, you children had better get home now, because it's getting late. You'd better get home."

Now when they saw your parents, they would want to know, "What time did the children get home?" (Children belonged to everybody then; your child was everybody's child.) "We told them to come home at such-and-such a time."

Or if you went somewhere else up the road, and you got to cutting up, they would come right out and say, "Now I know your mother and father don't know you're doing that. And I'm going to tell them. If you don't stop, I'm going to whip you."

There isn't love like that now.

And when we were boys, if those old folks were out hoeing the garden or pulling the grass out of the garden and we boys came along, we would go right over there, and sometimes we'd take the hoes away from the old folks and race to see who could pull the most grass.

The old people would help each other. They used to help each other. We called it packing together. Say I'm out on the bay in my boat, and I'm oystering here. Maybe there's two or three boats of us tonging here; maybe three or four over there. And those folks—some of them were church people—they'd sing at anything. Sometimes they hit a hymn out there and next thing you know, everybody grabs hold of it.

And maybe they are catching more oysters over there than we are over here. Then they'd say, "Why don't you come over here? We be doing pretty good over here."

And the next thing you know, we'd be over there; we'd all be packing together. Sometimes they'd sing that hymn "Gabriel is the man gonna blow out the sun." And if the Spirit came, everybody would get a piece of it. It got pretty good out there sometimes, when they got on one accord. Sometimes we'd catch loads of oysters and wouldn't feel tired. They used to pack together pretty good.

In those days, women mostly worked in the oyster-shucking houses, as the shuckers. There'd be plenty of music in those oyster houses. The women would get to singing and the shells would get to dropping on the floor. And they would sing up something in there; they would pack together just like the men would.

In the cornfields sometimes the old folks would sing a hymn, but it was nothing like in the oyster houses, because they'd start singing, and the next thing you know, there would be a race. You would go along singing and maybe four or five others would go around singing. And bye and bye, somebody would step out. The next thing you know he'd be fifteen or twenty rows ahead of you.

And you had to speed up, "Look at him; he's running, ain't he?"

Outside of Bellevue Seafood Company, a small oyster boat named *Amen* rests placidly in a creek off the Chesapeake.

10. "Blow, Gabriel"

A Straight Hymn

This notation is based on a performance of this hymn by the Eastern Shore Singing and Praying Band at Coolspring United Methodist Church, Girdletree, Maryland, on June 27, 1987. Rev. Edward Johnson of Ezion Methodist Church in Batt's Neck, Maryland, led the singing. The performance began with G as the tonic and at a tempo of 70 quarter notes per minute. At the conclusion of the hymn, the pitch had risen to A above middle C, and the tempo had increased to 106 quarter notes per minute. The pitch of the third varies; while usually it is a major third, occasionally it is sung flatted.

This song articulates a theme common among spirituals since the nineteenth century. Drawn from both the Book of Daniel and Revelation, it describes a moment at the end of time when the sun and moon cease to shine and the New Jerusalem will be lit by the light of God exclusively.

Return to chorus,
and proceed to
subsequent verses.

VERSES:

2. Give me a little time I'll talk it out right.
Tell you about the coming of Jesus Christ.

3. Paul he fell at the master's feet
Ananias told him to go and preach.

We wouldn't let him do that; he'd either stay in the group or we'd run him out of the field.

Those old folks used to do a lot of singing in those days. If you were in a field, you could hear them from one farm to another. It would sound good coming through there. In those days, when they cut the corn off, they'd make a shock eight rows apart. The bunches would be about eight rows apart. We used to call them shocks. And you carried the corn on your back to the bunch row where you make the bunches at. (You had to do it all by hand in those times.) They'd be out there all day. Sometimes they'd sing, sometimes they'd race to see who could cut the fastest. That old corn knife would go "tap! tap!" Sometimes it sounded like that corn knife was talking, like the sound from the corn knife fit right in with the singing. There was almost always somebody in the field who would make you laugh. If you beat me today, you would have to beat me tomorrow because I would come back at you tomorrow. They worked like that and everyone got along good.

And then you'd take two shocks and make one pile after you shucked the corn. You could go down the road and hear the corn falling and the people singing. They'd

Though the Chesapeake's oyster industry has declined sharply, the black-owned Bellevue Seafood Company in St. Michaels, Maryland, remained in business until the dawn of the twenty-first century.

sing and shuck and pitch it in a pile on the ground. They'd be singing one of those old hymns:

> What a great change since I've been born,
> People I used to see, I don't see no more.
> When I looked around, I saw death had been here.
> People I used to see, I don't see no more.

11. "People I Used to See"

A Straight Hymn

The musical notation presented below is based on a rendition of this hymn sung by the Eastern and Western Shore Singing and Praying Bands at John Wesley United Methodist Church in Liner's Road, Maryland, on June 9, 1985, led by Carrie Smith of Baltimore. The song began at a tempo of 68 quarter notes per minute, with E as the tonic note. During the course of the performance the tonic rose to A-sharp, and the tempo increased to 200 quarter notes per minute. The pitch of the third and sixth varies between flat and natural. This song is similar to one printed in Newman I. White's *American Negro Folk-songs*, pages 116–17:

> Been a great change since I been born,
> Things I used to do, I don't do now,
> Places I used to go, I don't go there now,
> Oh, people I used to see, I don't see 'em now.

It has been recorded by various gospel artists under the title "I Can't See 'Em Now."

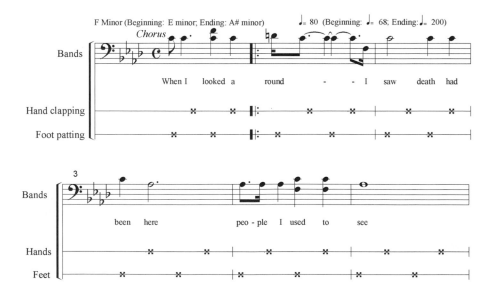

VERSES:

2. I feel my weakness every day.
Weakness tells me I must go away.

3. My poor mother, she oftime said
"What'ya gonna do, child, when I am dead?"

4. "What's that, Moses, you got in your hand?"
"Lord, it is my rod and staff."

5. What's the matter justice, can't you wait?
Four thousand years I'll meet you at the gate.

6. Look at the journey before you start
Won't take nothing but the pure of heart.

7. Let's go see, let's go see,
Let's go see what the end will be.

8. Gave me the witness, told me to go.
Gave me the trumpet, and he told me to blow.

9. Where you going, Gabriel, in the morning soon?
"Going down to blow out the sun and moon."

10. This old world is coming to an end.
What's gonna come of the wicked men?

11. Job, Job, where were you?
Old Job got in the kingdom too.

You could hear them for half a mile or so sometime, if the wind was fair, hear the corn—"pop! pop!"—hitting the ground. We used to go out there some moonlit nights and husk corn from about six or seven o'clock to about twelve that night. Sometimes on moonlit nights, they would shuck all night out there. And they would be singing. When they wouldn't be singing, they would be telling some kind of joke, telling lies, all kinds of lies, having a big laugh. People aren't like that now. It's different.

In the winter in Batt's Neck, instead of going to church and making a fire for singing and praying, they would go from house to house and have prayer service. Some of them had chairs in their homes, but some of them had only boxes all around the room to sit on. (Of course in those days many people didn't have good chairs like we have now.) And they would sit there, sing a hymn, have a prayer, have a shout, and get happy.

And those from Batt's Neck would walk from here to Matapeake for service. There used to be four or five families back there then. They would go to Stansbury's house tonight, for example. Maybe the night after that they'd go up to another Stansbury's house (there were two Stansbury brothers). And then they would stop at Old Man Frank Robinson's house another night. Then maybe the next week, those folks would come down to Batt's Neck, to these houses. And they'd go that way all winter.

And if you were sick, some of them would walk here to see you, eight or ten miles from Kent Point. Kent Point is about ten miles south of here. And people would walk from there to see you, "We've got to go see Sister So-and-so; we've got to go see her."

The way they would do it is this. If one is on a farm on this side of the road, maybe somebody else lives on the other side of the road on a farm. And the last one down, the one furthest down the road, would start out singing. And when he got up to the others' gates, they would be out there and join him, see. The next farm they would get up to, if there are people who live down there, why, they would come out and join in. And they would be singing together all the way from Kent Point up to the house. Sometimes there would be fifteen or sixteen people. And after they leave the house of whomever they had come to see, they all go out and get in the road and you could hear them for miles, going back down there singing, singing those old-time hymns. That's how they would get in touch with one another going and coming.

Just as Singing and Praying Band members sway when they sing, oyster shuckers seem to work in rhythm at Bellevue Seafood Company.

When I first got converted, I just felt all different. It was down here at Ezion Methodist Church here in Batt's Neck in 1928, during a preaching on Mother's Day. The district superintendent's wife—I forget her name now—preached a sermon that morning. And man, she *preached*. And when she got to preaching, she struck a hymn, an old song about:

> On Monday morning, he made me whole.
> If I could touch the hem of his garment
> His love would make me whole.

And she sang it all the way through from Monday to Sunday: the same line went from Monday to Sunday. And when I came to myself, they were helping me and sitting me down. I just felt all different. All that feeling of dread that you have sometimes, all the pains, you just feel like something has cleaned you out inside. Oh, man, it was a different feeling! You get light; you feel like you could fly away. A big change, I'm telling you. Converted! All the bad feelings go away.

And bye and bye, you come to yourself, and you realize that something has happened. I didn't realize it at first. But after I got settled, I realized I wasn't like I was before; I had a different mind and different attitude.

When I first started in the church, you had to be in church six months and you had to prove yourself. You had to walk as a Christian should. Then you'd have to grade up. They would see what you could take. "You're on probation now for six months. We want to show you now how to conduct yourself."

We used to have class meetings then, before preaching services. They would always have class leaders, maybe four or five men. Suppose you belonged to my class; the other leaders wouldn't call on you. But when my turn came up, then I'd call my class. Then you would get up and give your testimony or you could sing your hymn if you wanted. But you had to be prepared then.

And the class leader's responsibility was to see that you went right. Maybe you drank a little. Maybe you ran around a little bit, to different places, like house parties. If they saw you do anything they thought was wrong, he brought it to you and would tell you, "That doesn't become Christianity. You have to stop doing that."

They would test you. When they thought you were ripe, they would come to you and tell you, they used to call it "throw you overboard." They would tell you, "Ed, how about conducting class meeting next Sunday? How about singing the opening hymn for us next Sunday?"

See, they would give you the whole week to prepare. If you passed the test at home, and if you belonged to the Singing and Praying Band, they'd come to you,

Buster Wilson looks out over the line of fellow oyster shuckers the way a band captain might survey his sheep.

"We're going to such-and-such a place today. Do you think you can raise a hymn, sing a hymn? How about a prayer?"

When they thought I was ripe, they plucked me.

And this is what proved it: those that I used to associate with, they would bear off from me. "Oh, he belongs to the church," some of them said. "Ain't no fooling with him now, he belongs to the church."

But that never stopped me; I kept going.

My grandfather, my mother's father, was a slave to the man who had a farm by the airport there. I think his name was Tom, Big Tom Carvell. After he died his son took it over, and that's when they cut the slaves loose.

I heard the old folks talk afterwards about what they used to do when they got together. They would meet out there in the fields; sometimes they would meet out in the woods or in a shed and have their prayer meeting. They had to hide themselves to do it then. They would get together whenever they could; maybe four or five or six slaves would meet on Sundays.

I heard them say that they would put down stakes, and sometimes march around and around the stakes, sing and have a big time. They would be in the woods outside. Sometimes they would just draw a circle about six to eight feet in diameter and put a stake here, maybe a stake there, on the circumference of the circle. And instead of being on the inside, they'd be on the outside of the circle, marching. Marching to the right; they called it "the right way." The stakes represented the church. Sometimes they would take a box, a chair, anything to represent a church, and march around that. They'd draw a circle on the ground and then put stakes in and march all around. It stood for their church.

After freedom came, they would meet in each other's houses to have their services. They never had ministers come in until after slavery. They got freed and then they got together and got ministers to come in. And the Singing and Praying Bands started right after slavery; that's when the bands came in.

In those times, they didn't have camp meetings like we have them now. They would move in right down there on the grounds, down there at this church here, clear the place back in the woods, put up a tent, bring out some cots, and they would stay there from the time it started until it ended. They stayed right there on that ground for a week or two weeks.

The way the Singing and Praying Bands did it is, they would go and help each other. If you come to help me, then when you have your camp meeting, I'll come and help you. That's a pretty good way because if you were not invited there to help them and they never came to help you, you would be divided all the time. If you come into contact with one another, you could learn from one another.

And so people would come there from all places. The two churches in Grasonville, each one of them had a Singing and Praying Band. Carmichael, Butlertown, and Price, and over there in Denton, East New Market, Ridgely, Marion Station, Marydel, all of those fellows had bands that used to come over here. And they wouldn't do like they do now and have food there to sell. At that time, they would bring baskets of food and they would go out there and camp and sing and pray. And when eating time came everybody shared. When they got through, they would go on back home. That's where camp meeting comes from.

That was a special time, camp time. Sometimes people would come riding in farm wagons. They would take two horses to a wagon, put boards across the wagons and make seats; they'd put straw in the bottom, put the children and things in the bottom, and they'd sit on the seats. When they got about a mile from the church, you could listen, you could hear them come. When they got there, they already had the fire burning. Some of them would be getting off the wagon shouting, singing and shouting.

Sometimes when the Broadneck band would come to Batt's Neck camp, they would bring a hundred, a hundred and fifty people. They used to come across the bay in little work boats—oyster boats—and land up here at Wilsontown, up there by Matapeake. Then they would walk down to church here. And when their band was on the floor, there wasn't any room for any other band. And they used to come down here the last Sunday evening of our camp and they wouldn't leave until that

Monday morning. On Monday morning, they would sing from this church all the way to Matapeake, where they would get back on the boats to cross the bay.

At a camp meeting, two bands might march in at once, and the band that leads off might sing a hymn and a prayer and then the captain would raise another hymn and he'd march out on that. And the band behind him would continue singing that. And the captain of the second band would go down in prayer, and then he would raise a hymn. And then a third band would march in on his hymn. In that way, all of the bands had a chance.

When they start singing, the Spirit isn't there; it's mostly dry. Maybe after they give out a verse or two, you can feel the difference in the singing. And about the time they get to the middle of the hymn, that's when they've *got* it. Everybody is packing together, you see, and everybody shouts at the same time, and there's a real uprising in the church. Then again, maybe a captain calls on somebody to pray, and the spirit of that prayer runs from one to another; the next thing you know they'll be shouting and everything.

Everybody shouts together. That's what "one accord" means. "On one accord" means we're all striving for the same place and for the same thing. We blend our thoughts together, point them to the same place. Isaiah says that there's a highway to heaven, and none can walk there but the redeemed of the Lord [Isa. 35:8 9], and the road is narrow, but it is straight [Matt. 7:14].

"We blend our thoughts together, point them to the same place." Mary Hunt seems in touch with a sublime presence during a service at Antioch A.M.E. Church, Frankford, Delaware.

A moment later, Mary Hunt comforts Patricia Hunt, at Antioch A.M.E.

When one person shouts, others rush over to help.

As the Spirit runs from heart to heart and breast to breast, Elva Tongue of Annapolis shouts, and Marlon Hall, Rosie Walters, and Shawn Copeland come to her aid.

A hand of comfort reaches out as the Spirit comes onto Alfred Green.

Orlando Purnell raises an open palm during a peak moment of a band service.

Sometimes people would get happy and turn the benches over. So, up to ten or fifteen years ago, if the band was big, they moved the church benches back so the band would have room. And when the bands commenced, they would either get the sinners to convert or make them get out of there, one or the other. It would be so hot in church, they had to do something: either come to the Lord, or go.

Now I'll tell you one thing. Very few converts come into the church through preaching. Sometimes a preacher would get a convert, but it wasn't like the converts at camp, because when they came through with their conversion at camp meeting, they would come through singing and shouting.

My band from Ezion Church in Batt's Neck used to break camp at Broadneck. That would be our duty. We'd leave Batt's Neck on Sunday evening after our church service, and we'd go over there. We might sing over there on Sunday evening. But it used to always be our duty to sing after midnight preaching service and then again in the morning. At four o'clock, they would start class meeting. And as soon as that was over, they called the bands together saying, "Let's start our march."

And then they would march all the way around Broadneck campground, the whole length of the grounds. And when they started marching, I've seen as many as fourteen or fifteen head get converted right out on that ground. It was very seldom that they had camp meeting then that they didn't get some converts.

In those days, some of the bands had thirty-five or forty head in the band. At Magothy, they would sometimes have four or five bands outside singing, from the time you get there on Sunday until that Monday morning.

One time we were there, we started that Monday morning at 4:00 A.M. on that final night of the camp meeting and never sang but one hymn. We raised that one hymn, started marching on it, and we stayed there until 11:00 A.M. When we left there, these other bands had grabbed it and they were singing that same hymn: "I've been praying so long / Satisfied, my Lord, satisfied."

And I mean, it was hot. You could walk around that ground and feel the cold chills run over you.

We left at 11:00 A.M. I had to go get my people and tell them, "We've got to go. We've got to go."

And they were still shouting. They didn't want to leave that hymn.

12. "Satisfied, My Lord, Satisfied"

A Straight Hymn

The musical notation presented below is based on a version of this song given by George Beckett of Frankford, Delaware, during an interview at his home on May 24, 1999. The pitch of the third (the note D) varies, sometimes sung as a minor third, sometimes a major, and at other times oscillating between the two.

When a person who belonged to the bands dies, the band always has the last say at the funeral. The preacher preaches the funeral, and after he gets through, they turn it over to the bands, and the band members have a say. Each captain or band member gets up and either sings a hymn or talks about how he was. Sometimes they just stand at their seats; sometimes the bands come forward and surround the casket, and each will have something to say or to sing. Then they raise a hymn as a group and march out. If the graveyard is close, they walk to the grave. They sing all the way to the grave, sing a straight hymn like:

No longer needing to meet secretly in the woods for their prayer meeting, as worshippers did in slavery times, band members form a circle and sing in the fellowship hall at Magothy.

See you again, see you again,
See you in that day,
March along, march along,
See you in that day.

When they would get down to the grave, after the preacher reads his part, one of them would pray a prayer and they would start a hymn and sing until they lower him into the grave.

Back in the old days, they clung to everybody more than they do now. I mean, in those times, at a funeral, you just *had* to be there. Just *had* to be there. It's like that old hymn says:

Together let us sweetly live,
Together let us die;
And each a starry crown receive,
And reign above the sky.

If we don't get together, then we don't receive the starry crown. People didn't mind helping you then, and everybody got along good. They don't do that now.

13. "March Along, March Along"

A Straight Hymn

The notation below is based on a version of the song "March Along" that was sung by Cordonsal Walters in the home of Elizabeth Hall, Millsboro, Delaware, during a personal interview on July 7, 1998. The pitch of the third varies between F-natural and F-sharp.

VERSE:

2. Gonna take a tedious journey,
Who you gonna take along with you?
See you again, see you again.
Gonna take a tedious journey,
Who you gonna take along with you?
See you in that day.

SIX

Cordonsal Walters
(b. 1913)

Circles always seemed to be the instigator of prayer meeting.

MY FATHER'S MOTHER was a little slave girl; she was a little slave girl. Her name was Adeline, but they called her Ad. She was from Guyana—or maybe Guinea—I can't tell you definitely where she came from. But she came to Delaware by way of the beach. The boat came in down near Fenwick Island, and they settled in Sussex County.

When the Emancipation Proclamation was signed, the lady of the family that owned her had chickens that laid eggs under the house. She was a small child. She had to crawl under the house and get these eggs.

And the lady, her slave master, said, "I don't know what I'm going to do when you leave."

She told me that more than once. "I don't know what I'm going to do when you leave," because she didn't have anybody to go under the house and get the eggs.

She was a little girl. She told me that several times.

She was a camp-meeting person. She talked the year around about camp meetings.

Cordonsal Walters punctuates an old family story by pointing emphatically with the tip of his index finger.

They had a bigger shout in slavery times than they have now. They would have prayer meetings in the cabins, or anywhere. They would shout outside and they would shout coming on the road home from church. They would shout anywhere they hit the spirit. I heard that from my grandfather, Caleb Walters. My father's name was George D. Walters. My mother's name was Angela Walters. My whole family was prayer-meeting people. My home church was Union Wesley in Clarksville; that was my root-and-branch church.

I remember camp meetings in horse-and-buggy days. They used to drive horse and buggies to camp. They would take the horse from the wagon, feed him, and get water, especially if they were going to be there all day (you'd see some pretty horses!). There used to be covered wagons; they didn't have any cabins. People would stay in those covered wagons for two weeks, just like we stay in these tents. After covered wagons, they commenced building tents; they built the tents out of wood because it was cheaper and handier.

Ever since I was born, each church had a prayer-meeting band. Prayer meeting was the last part of the service. Service started with a testimony service, went to preaching, and then after the preacher came the prayer bands. Each church—like Frankford, Clarksville, Berlin, Johnson's Neck—had a prayer-meeting band with ten or twelve members. They used to band together when they had their big days. That's the reason camp meetings came about. This program we've got now includes Delaware and Maryland. It's a union. It seems to me prayer meetings and camp meetings went hand in hand.

The same way they helped one another going from church to church, they did farming. In other words, if you had your corn in, your neighbor would help you and you would help him. They did it year in and year out; it would be five or six farms, maybe a dozen farms. They helped one another: help them plant, help them reap. It was just a family affair.

Harvesting corn was done three different ways. The first way, you started by cutting the tops of the corn stalk, right above the ears of corn. After they cut the tops off, they would strip blades from the same stalk. A blade would be a leaf from the corn plant. They wouldn't touch that ear. You put the blades under your arm until

At Union Wesley Church in Clarksville, Delaware, an outdoor wooden tabernacle surrounded by wooden tents and cottages is the center of camp-meeting activities.

you got a big bundle, then you would tie them up and stick them between two hills of corn, about every twenty rows.

Then after they got that done, everybody worked to "pull the blades." That is, the men would come by and pick them up and carry them up to the barn. They'd fill the barn first and when they had too much, they put them in a stack, outside the barn or out in the field. Those people could stack the tops and blades so that they wouldn't rot, and they wouldn't even leak. That stack could stay there up to two years if they wanted it.

They stood the bundles of tops up on end around a pole, about five foot from the pole all around. And they would lay bundles of tops on top of other tops; the tops would be stacked about four or five feet high. Then they would put their blades on top of this here first foundation. They would carry that up so high they couldn't get any higher, then they'd cap it off with tops. The tops would be hanging over the side of the stack. They could make the fodder stacks look like these Chinese houses that you've seen in books, or like a gazebo. So that was the secret of stacking. They could do some the prettiest work you have ever seen.

The latter part of August is when they used to begin harvesting their fodder and tops. When they cut the tops off, they'd let the corn and the stalk be. And then, after the first frost fall, after letting the corn dry, they used to commence shucking corn right there in that field. They shucked it with a corn peg. They'd throw the ears of corn on the ground in piles. Then the men would come around in his wagon and pick up the corn and carry it to the barn. When they got all the corn shucked, they'd get it into the corn crib (in the old days, they had a grinder to shell the corn from the cob, turned by hand). And they used the bottoms of the stalk for bedding around the pens, around the stables and all. The corn and the fodder would go to the owner of the farm and the man that was sharecropping, the owner of the farm and the tenant. If the tenant furnished the whole team to pull the wagon, it was divided half-and-half. If the owner of the ground furnished the team, the tenant would get a third. But the tenant did all the work anyhow.

They stopped doing all that work. That was just working them to death. Oh, that's work, work, work, work. Those folks worked themselves to death for nothing.

In later years, the more modern way to do it was shucking the corn, the blades, the tassels, and the tops together. They were all one thing. They cut it down and put it in a shock in August and September. The blades would be just turning tannish. After they cut it down, there was no sap going up, and the fodder was going to cure anyway. The corn would also cure. They called it shock fodder. After a while it dried out.

After the first frost, they'd go down there and turn the shocks over and commence shucking corn, shucking the ears out. They'd have about five or six bushels from one pile, six or eight bushels in one pile. Then they would shock the stalks back like they were, after the corn was out. If they didn't have a place up in the barn to put the fodder, they would leave it right in the field, the same stack; this was a "shock stack." They could leave it out there till they needed it. They would try to be done shucking the corn by Thanksgiving.

This is the primitive way, what I told you. The third way, after they stopped shocking, the machinery took over. And when the modern tractors and thrashers and corn shuckers took over, the work was cut in half. I'm going to say that was in 1929 or the early 1930s. But whatever there was to do, they would do it together. The same dozen farms would be there together; they'd all work together from on the thresher.

Anytime between Thanksgiving and Christmas was hog-killing time. And that's also when everybody helped one another out. They raised great big hogs weighing three hundred and four hundred pounds. They could do a half a dozen in one day. And you talk about some pretty meat!

An old-time hog killing would be something to see. They started off early in the morning; the sun would be rising. They scalded the hog in a barrel of boiling water. They put the hindquarters in the barrel first. Then they'd turn him over with the hooves standing up out of that hot water (the head was always harder to get off than the body parts). When you could wring the hair off of him with your hands, he was ready to come out.

You would get a hog pole, put it on the ground, open his legs wide, put that pole

A fire stand, a replica of a covered wagon, and a concession stand greet visitors traveling the dirt road to Union Wesley's campground.

right between that hog's legs, hook that hook in the back of the hooves, pick the pole up, and put that hog right up there in that old forked tree. You hung him up and let him air out just a few minutes.

The next thing, they would take the intestines out. Some people could take the intestines out of a hog in three minutes. When the sun got up there in the morning, there would be two or three hogs hanging up there, washed down just as pretty as you want to see.

They'd cut it into hams, shoulders, middlins. The bacon was the middlin—that's part of the ribs. They had some knives that they only kept for hog-killing time. They were wrapped up for a whole year. They had some knives that could shave anything. They'd cut that thing up in nothing flat.

The men did the killing and the cleaning and the women took the intestines and chitterlings and made sausage and scrapple. *My dear,* you are talking about something good! The tenderloin meat was some of the best meat you'd ever have. They used to cook that meat—just fried it almost done—and put it in these quart jars, press that grease in on top of it when it was hot, put the lid on, tighten that lid, turn it upside down, and that stuff would keep for years and years (and sausage—they'd do sausage that way too). You never got any of that until strawberry time. That was the time they would be busy working in the strawberry fields. It was a quick meal; it was already cooked, you know.

They smoked the ham and the shoulders and the middlins. They would put salt on it before they smoked it, because the smoke was the finishing touch. They'd make a fire in the smokehouse. They got hickory wood and they had an iron pot that they'd make a fire in the middle of the smokehouse; they put this oak or hickory in there, and they'd have a pile of dirt around the kettle to keep from setting the smokehouse on fire. The meat would be in there hanging up. Sometimes, you'd see smoke pouring out of there like a fire. The smoke would go into the meat. If the wind was right, you could smell that meat one hundred yards before you got to the house. (*My dear,* you could make a man hungry!)

And then after they smoked it, they would wrap it up in paper and bags and hang it up in the smokehouse. That's how they kept it, their meat.

They had fun killing hogs. And you talk about food to eat: when the liver came out of that hog, that's the best time to eat it. It was the first thing they hung up. They washed it, and the blood dripped and dripped and dripped, and when it came to lunchtime, you saw those ladies come up there and take whatever part of that liver they wanted to cut. And they knew just how to season it.

Everybody made wine. Peach, they used to make, or wild cherry (and my mother used to make some good apple jack). Hog-killing time was when they got the wine out. *Good God Almighty!* But you never saw anybody get drunk. They had work to do and they would do it. I've seen them get feeling good and happy, and get the hog cleaned up, and they'd be dancing, buck dancing.

Years ago, when I was a real young boy, they didn't have any dancing in our A.M.E. camp. They didn't have it. But they would include shouting. You were dancing for the devil if you crossed your legs; it was a sin. So people never crossed their feet when singing in the bands. That's what kept it sacred. If they crossed their feet, it wasn't sacred.

Old people years ago used to start out a prayer meeting with a book hymn like "My hope is built on nothing less than Jesus' blood and righteousness." Sometimes they would line it out and then they would sing it. In some churches, they'd sing sitting in the pews. And then again, in another church they would stand right where the seats were, clap their hands, shout, and get right with it.

And while they were singing the book hymn, they would march up front and make a circle. The book hymn was to round them up; they came up front while singing the book hymn. After they went down in prayer, somebody would have something to say. Then prayer meeting would take over. They'd start this new type of singing, a straight hymn, a piece like:

> Ain't no grave gonna hold my body in that day.
> Ain't no grave gonna hold my body in that day.
> When Gabriel gets ready to blow,
> I'm gonna get up in the morning and go.
> Ain't no grave gonna hold my body in that day.

That type of piece goes back to when I was a boy. That would be the drawing card. As soon as they change that key, they were gone. Yes, sir, they'd start out in a circle: sing in a circle, pray in a circle, march in a circle. Circles always seemed to be the instigator of prayer meeting.

And they didn't stand still; they marched in a ring. It was always counterclockwise, just like they march around here today. They got it from this story about when "Joshua marched the Jericho 'round. / The Israelites shouted and the walls fell down." And that was such a success that people are still trying it!

They had some beautiful pieces back then. Mr. Charles Beckett, Ben Beckett's grandfather, used to sing,

> Stand the storm; it won't be long.
> Stand the storm; it won't be long.
> Stand the storm; it won't be long.
> And we'll anchor in the harbor bye and bye.

That's a song they say came from slavery; that's a *bad* piece. "Over on the other side of Jordan, where the tree of life is blooming" was my father's piece.

In a maneuver common to ring shouts throughout the United States, band members begin their march around Jericho by marching in a counterclockwise direction around the mourners' bench.

14. "Over on the Other Side of Jordan"

A Straight Hymn

Katherine Marine of Harrisville, Maryland, led the Eastern Shore Singing and Praying Band in singing the rendition of this hymn presented in notation below, recorded at Lane United Methodist Church on Taylors Island, Maryland, on August 6, 2000. This performance began with a tonic of B below middle C, at a tempo of 76 quarter notes per minute. It concluded with the tonic having risen to C-sharp, and the tempo accelerated to 110 quarter notes per minute.

When the bands perform this hymn, they sing the chorus through and add verses, as is their custom for straight hymns. When they get ready to march, however, they sing a truncated form of the chorus and change the melody into a repetitive chant to which it is easier to march. In this example, the truncated chant is noted as the coda. The first three lines of the hymn seem to derive from the hymn "Rest for the Weary," by William Hunter (1811–77).

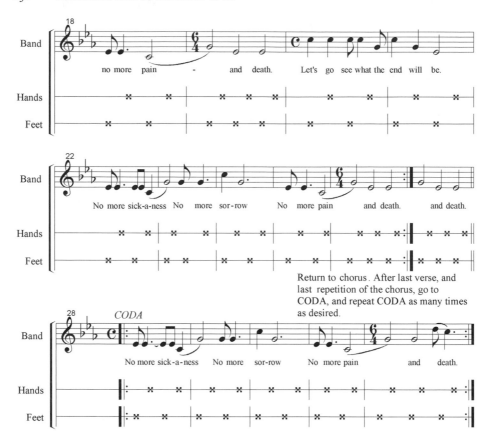

Return to chorus. After last verse, and
last repetition of the chorus, go to
CODA, and repeat CODA as many times
as desired.

VERSES:

2. My poor mother she oftimes said,
What'cha gonna do, child, when I am dead.

3. Choose a robe and try it on.
If it fits you, wear it home.

4. They hung him high and they stretched him wide.
That is the way my savior died.

5. I feel my weak-a-ness everyday.
Weak-a-ness tells me I must go away.

And "Same train took my mother" is a pretty piece:

Same train took my mother,
Same train took my mother,
Same train took my mother
Gonna take you and I someday.

They were singing that piece when I was a little boy. I call it the death train, because death is so prevalent in the land. It doesn't miss anybody: father, mother, sister, brother. It could have been an underground railroad song. But we didn't emphasize that or think of it in that way.

I don't know who wrote them—the kind of thing people composed never got written down. It used to be that everybody had a song and they'd get together and practice it and they'd sing it and nobody thought too much about it. Later, it became a great song, maybe.

You put into a straight hymn just whatever verses come into your mind. Why, I can start from Genesis and I can go pretty near any book in that Bible I want to take a verse out of. *Lord, have mercy!* But if you are singing about the book of Revelation, there is no need of putting in a verse about "Joshua marched the Jericho 'round." You put in verses according to what you're preaching about, teaching about. A lot of people didn't know how to read back in those days that had these beautiful songs.

The faithful who attend Union Wesley's July camp meeting listen raptly to a preaching service before they rise from their seats and begin their prayer meeting.

But they would listen. They listened to these Bible stories. The Bible won't rhyme, though. We make the rhyming up among ourselves by singing. That helped them remember. You use two lines that would rhyme to balance your piece:

Just look a yonder what my Lord done,
Decorated the heavens and hung out the sun.

And I put in about:

Sinner man swinging on the gates of hell,
Gate give way and the sinner man fell.

I picked them up going to churches and camp meetings, from my father, from generations long ago, and I picked some up from the radio way back. There's a lady in Millsboro who is full of verses. I got so many from her. It is something that comes

Youngsters play in the attic window of a camp-meeting cottage, while adults attend to their spiritual affairs in the tabernacle nearby.

if you remember the Sunday school lessons the way you were taught: it'll come to you naturally. People make verses out of those kinds of subjects; we're educating people about the Old Testament and the New.

Shouting is a spiritual happening. They start out in a circle, clapping right from the start, and they clap their hands the whole time. You carry your time with your hands. You lean forward a bit, flexing the knees (you can be straight if you want, but it's easier for me to lean over). Some of them are patting their feet. You alternate your feet, patting first one foot, then the other. This heel comes up. Every time the foot moves up, my hand hits. I clap my hands when *this* knee flexes; I clap my hands when *this other* knee flexes. You see, every time my hands beat together, there's one foot going down and another coming up. This is what you call a motion.

You don't have to move your feet. You can motion just from your knees, just flexing your knees. You can stand up and just flex your legs from your thighs. When you flex your knees, alternating with the clapping, you can stand still. But you're doing it with both knees at a time.

It's a *motion*; you do it according to your feelings. Just do whatever feels good to you. These men from the Baltimore area motion from side to side. When they go to that side they clap; then they turn to the other side and clap. Whatever way they turn, they just keep clapping. That's an alternate motion. The motion with the knees is just the same.

Everybody has practically their own style. Old Gus would fly sometimes, take the wings of the morning and fly away. When Gus was getting ready to throw in a verse sometimes, that would be the sign for them to listen to his verse (Old Gus was a *bad* man!). A lot of people motion with a bow; I call it giving reverence. There are a lot of people who bow. And when some people go to put in a verse, they'll hold their hands up and that gives the sign they're going to add a verse: your particular verse and your particular motion.

If I go put in a verse, I'll get in the middle. The man in the middle of the circle is the leader. When I'm going to verse a piece, I might clap double time. I double up on the clapping. Instead of patting both feet, I use one foot. The right foot is my drum; that's my drum. I keep the same time with my feet, but I double up on my hand clapping.

With a *march*, everybody's walking their bodies in time. They call it a Christian walk. Everybody's in line or side by side, and they're going one way. Some people will motion with the march.

A *shout* is a jump that you do from your toes. An ordinary jump you do from your heels. People had different techniques, but the good shouters were on their toes. I like to do the toe jump; it seems to me to be more appropriate.

It's the same step as the motion: you flex your knees. You're motioning with your knees, but it grows into a jump. Your body would be going through the same motion,

Waving his arms like an eagle might flap its wings, Gus Bivens steps into the center of the ring of singers and adds a verse to a straight hymn.

As observers have reported shouters doing since the nineteenth century, Zarek Brown jumps off the floor and twirls in a counterclockwise direction when he is smitten by the Spirit.

but you're not just doing it with part of your body; you're doing it with all of your body. I've seen people shout and you could hardly hear them touch the floor.

Some people *shouted* differently from others. People had different techniques, just like motioning. You just do whatever feels good to you. Some people shout and glide; I've seen a woman who could shout in church and it looked like she was gliding, just gliding across the floor. It did seem she was jumping just on her toes, but I don't know how she did it.

I used to be a good dancer. Since I've come to Christianity, I don't put the steps of dancing in this service as I put when I was dancing with a woman, or tap dancing. I've seen people dance in the Spirit, I guess. But when I danced out there in the world, I was in another spirit. Now, I do a *religious walk*. There's more harmony; it's more sophisticated. That's the only thing that's different.

SEVEN

Susanna Watkins
(1905–99)

There's no use standing up in the band if you are not going to help.

I BELONG TO THIS GROUP OF PEOPLE, the Sandtown group. My parents were all from Calvert County. My husband, my father, and my grandfather, all of them were from Calvert County. All of them. But I was born here in Baltimore, on Bruce Street, over there between Fulton Avenue and Pressman Street. And that was considered what we called Sandtown. We couldn't live on Baker Street because at that time it was all white people in that neighborhood. They were Sandtown too, but they didn't act Sandtown. But *my* group was called Sandtown.

My church, that's Ames Memorial, is on the corner of Carey and Baker Street in West Baltimore. That's where I got my husband, Judge, from. I used to go to the six o'clock class meeting on Sunday mornings and there's where Judge was out there singing. His father and my father played together in Calvert County. (Of course, Judge is from my people's home. And his father and my father were playmates. So they knew one another.)

And I was just sitting there six o'clock Sunday morning. And I said to myself, "Now you see, that's the man I'm going to marry." I said that.

And he had an aunt that loved him like he was a little baby. Crazy about him. And she said to me once, "Why don't you come by? Why don't you come to my house sometime?"

And I said, "No, I don't think . . . unless I'm invited by this man."

So he told his aunt about me. And his aunt came to church and said, "My nephew said he invited you to the house." And she said that "I love my nephew," she said, "and you are welcome to come."

And I went there, and Judge became my husband.

And my husband was band captain until the Lord claimed him. And I was captain for the women for about fifteen or eighteen years.

At Ames, we had a whole week of camp meeting. We started out on Monday, and I would run a week's meeting from Monday to Sunday. We had preaching every night through the week, and testimony. And we closed out on Sunday, the fourth Sunday in September every year. We called it Calvert County Day, because, you see, most of the people of Ames were from Calvert County.

A dignified Susanna Watkins sits in her wheelchair and recounts how she and her husband, Judge, organized the camp meetings at Ames United Methodist Church in Baltimore.

And Sisters' Night was on Friday night. That was a big night. Every activity we had, the women would take charge of by leading it. In other words, we did the presiding.

We would have *good* women preachers. And it was beautiful. But it was not as large as the last Sunday because people would come for Calvert County Day, our big Sunday.

And Sunday, we had to get a police permit and we blocked the street off from Pennsylvania Avenue down there up to my church. And the buses would park from my church on Carey and Baker up to Calhoun Street. And the people from Calvert County would come, all over the city would come, and we had, without exaggerating, we had about ten or twelve buses from Calvert County, Philadelphia, the Eastern Shore; and the people from Washington, Delaware, all of them would come. And we had a *big* day.

I would have a preacher at eleven o'clock in the morning. And then I would have another one at 3:00 P.M. The Eastern Shore Bands would come and sing after the morning service, and then in the afternoon, they would sing again. And then, after that, I would have night service.

We had bands all day. We had preaching upstairs in the sanctuary and we had choirs from different churches and band people from different churches, and they were all upstairs. I was downstairs in the fellowship hall doing all the cooking. I was the cook. We sold dinners, dinners of all kinds. The preacher would be upstairs

Women in the bands have always had their chance to preside. On her knees before the mourners' bench, Carrie Smith leads a prayer at Mt. Zion in Magothy, Maryland.

preaching, see. Then after he finished preaching, the band would start singing up-stairs. Then the band would march downstairs to continue singing for the people who were in the hall. Or after preaching, they marched upstairs and marched all around the church. Then, they would march downstairs again. But you could not get all of them downstairs. So some were downstairs singing and some were upstairs singing. There would be that many people.

And then before the preacher would leave, we had another service. So they would march upstairs and sit and hear him preach. Then the bands started off again and marched downstairs. All of them would go downstairs. And that's where we would end up.

The bands could march out on the pavement; they were allowed to do that. They could sing band pieces right out there if they wanted to. Outside, the younger men of the church sold soft drinks on the pavement; they sold ice cream and things like that.

And we had police protection because the other people in the neighborhood would open up their houses and they would sell food on the street. The money wasn't given to us; they were keeping the money. So we would have police there to stop them from that, because it was not for the church. And that meeting would not close out until about twelve or one o'clock at night.

After cooking all day in a camp-meeting concession stand, Raymond Hill Jr. (right) relaxes with fellow vendors Craig (left) and LaShell Green (center) at a table set up for their customers.

And when that Sunday was over, and I went to make my report, we made over six or seven hundred dollars from that day alone because it was an all-day meeting. That's why the band has a day. We had a *big* day. It was an old tradition that people used to have years ago. We had it for years and years.

On communion Sundays, Ames band marched up to communion in a group. Judge had charge of the men and I had charge of the sisters. And after everyone else had communed, we would march forward singing one of those old-time hymns. We would sing whatever came into our minds, maybe something like "A Charge to Keep I Have." And when we would march up, the men would go up one aisle, and the women would come up the other. You know how our band people cut up, crying and shouting? Our church would be on hallelujah fire; they just waited for that, because they liked that old-time hymn.

The women had on blue uniform dresses and white aprons. The collars of the dresses were white. And what we had were little blue hats with a little white band around it that was the color of our dresses. The men had on their band coats, which were either brown or black. The coat they wore in the band, that's what they went to communion in. And years ago, we all wore badges. If I was the captain, I would have one that said "Ames."

Mary Stewart and Ricky Bailey and the congregation seated behind them succumb to "hallelujah fire" when the bands march at Antioch in Frankford, Delaware.

Then when we got to the altar, we would kneel for prayer. Judge and the men knelt on one side of the altar, and we knelt on the other side. And then we would commune. Then when that was over, we would sing another hymn coming back down the aisle. The church was on fire.

Watch night—that was the last day of the year—was a night when almost everybody in the church had a part. People would come in from late at night, many people who never did come to church. We didn't care if you were a saint or a sinner; you could come in. But if you came in and you were under the influence of liquor, the ushers sat you in the back. And if you got unruly, they would say very nicely, "Come on, you can't stay in, but if you act nicely, okay."

They would have preaching and they would have class meeting, and everybody that could talk, talked: "thank God for this," and "thank God for that." That was a big night. At twelve o'clock, everybody would be down on their knees. And then we got up singing, "What a happy New Year." We would sing that:

What a happy New Year.
What a happy New Year.
What a happy, what a happy,
What a happy New Year.

Composing her thoughts before she starts, Mary Randall begins a prayer at Union Chapel A.M.E. Church near Cambridge, Maryland.

After that, the Singing and Praying Band would get together and sing—not too long, but we would have a *good* time. And then some churches had it longer. There, we would sing until daybreak.

And then, I would invite the men whose wives had died to my house on New Year's Day. Once upon a time, you did not let a woman walk into your house first in the new year. She didn't come in, not in our house, not in anybody's house. They say she was bad luck. A man always had to enter our house first. He was considered to be good luck to your house. And so I would have that group of men who didn't have wives to my house. So I had *good* luck. And they were as nice as they could be. I always had a big dinner, black-eyed peas, ham, collard greens. And after they ate that, they would walk all through my house, in every room, bless every room, walk through every room I had, and I had five. And they went through every room.

We had a preacher here in West Baltimore that used to go out in the street and preach. He was a Baptist preacher. And he had a little Ford. And the top of the Ford would turn back. He went out trying to, what they used to call years ago sinner hunting. And he would get out of his car and stand in the middle of the street and preach, kneel down in the street and pray. Or he would turn the top back in his car, and he would sit up there and sing. He would sing ballad hymns and then you could buy the ballad hymns from him. When we got them, they were on a piece of paper. Now that hymn that Mary Louise Chester used to sing, "O Tell Me Where Is the Gambling Man," now that was a ballad hymn. He sang that.

And on my block, at one time, men used to shoot craps. And play cards. And when that man would drive in there with that car, they would sit on the steps and listen attentively to what he used to say.

> ### Excerpts from "The Gambler"
>
> Tell me where is the gambling man,
> where is he gone?
> Where is the gambling man, pray tell
> me where is he gone?
>
> Boys, you always stood by me
>   In every kind of game,
> And if you go and leave me now,
>   You ought to be ashamed.
> A friend turned and looked at him,
>   Then said, "Oh well,
> I believe you are going to die,
>   I am sure you are going to hell."
>
> Then he began to grow so weak
>   His friends began to shake,
> He said to the man that ran the game,
>   "I now see your mistake.
> I always thought I was a fool,
>   My conscience told me so,
> While I was trying to beat someone
>   The Devil has won my soul."
> . . . .
> Now friends these are my dying words,
>   I want you all to know
> That death has laid his hands on me.
>   I am not prepared to go,
> Yes, that little black train
>   And devils are standing by my side,
> And hell is the very first station—
>   Oh my Lord, what a miserable ride.

And then when he passed his hat, they would put money in that hat and they didn't do one thing as long as he was in there; that was service. I was a girl then. I was sitting on my mother's steps. And when he would come in the block, everybody was silent. Nobody would move.

There was a man who had a church down there in south Baltimore and he would march his band out in the street. They would march out on the street the last of their camp. It would be a big band; twenty-five or thirty-five people marched. He would march them around the block to let people know what they were doing. And they had their aprons on and all, and they would stop in the middle of the street and pray, kneel down, just like we did in church. And then they would get up and sing and march again. Marching around Jericho's walls. Sometimes they would stay on the block for an hour and a half or two hours, according to the way the people would be. And somebody would take a hat and take up a little collection, and the people on the steps would put some money in it for you.

　　And they had a yard. And after we sang in the church, and he brought us into the street and marched us around the block, then they sang in the yard. It was nice like that too, a nice service.

Orlando Purnell, Marlon Hall, Cliff Williams, and Harrison Tindley (foreground, left to right) lead a march in the street in front of Mt. Zion at Magothy, Maryland.

The purpose of the Singing and Praying Bands is to help each other. That's all there is. What I mean by "help" is, for instance, if you are kneeling down there and you are praying, and you say, "Oh Lord . . . ," then the other people repeat the same thing you said. You see, that's strengthening to you.

If I say, "And am I born to die, to lay this body down," you say, "Must my trembling spirit fly . . ."

15. "And Am I Born to Die?"

A Give-out Hymn

The notation below is based on a recording of a performance of this hymn by the Eastern Shore Singing and Praying Band at Asbury Town Neck United Methodist Church on July 19, 1998, led by Catherine Ennels of Cambridge, Maryland. The text was written by Charles Wesley (1707–88). As with other band hymns, the singing began slowly, at a low pitch, and rose steadily throughout the performance. At the beginning the tempo was 36 quarter notes per minute, but at the end it had reached 94 quarter notes per minute. Also, while the performance began with F as the tonic note, at the conclusion of the singing the tonic had risen to G.

VERSES:

2. A land of deepest shade, unpierced by human thought,
The dreary regions of the dead, where all things are forgot.

3. Soon as from earth I go, what will become of me?
Eternal happiness or woe must then my portion be.

4. Waked by the trumpet's sound, I from my grave shall rise
And see the judge, with glory crowned, and see the flaming skies.

5. Who can resolve the doubt that tears my anxious breast?
Shall I be with the damned cast out, or numbered with the blest?

6. I must from God be driven, or with my Savior dwell,
Must come at his command to heaven, or else depart to hell.

7. O thou who wouldst not have one wretched sinner die,
Who diedst thyself my soul to save from endless misery.

8. Show me the way to shun thy dreadful wrath severe
That when thou comest on thy throne, I may with joy appear.

9. I have a crown laid up for me, a crown that will not fade;
The righteous judge in that great day shall place it on my head.

In the bands, each member helps the others by pulling together like the oarsmen of a boat, until they get on one accord.

That's how we do it, helping each other. That's the purpose of it. There's no use standing up in the band if you are not going to help. If I am giving out a hymn or something, they say, "Come on, Susanna."

See, that's the band; that's band singing. I couldn't do it by myself.

We helped each other by singing and praying together. There's a hymn we sing; I give it out all the time:

Help us to help each other, Lord,
Each other's cross to bear.
Let each his friendly aid afford
And feel his brother's care.

You can't just sing on your own. After a while they are singing with so much spirit in them because they are singing to help. That's right, they are getting the Spirit, helping each other.

And what the bands have always done is, we will visit each other. If Magothy had a camp meeting for a whole week, we lived in Magothy. Likewise, we had to go to all the churches that had camp meeting, to help the captain who helped you. You come to my camp and I'll go to yours. He helped you, so you have got to go to help him. That's what kept the camp meeting going. We support each other. That was our purpose. And that's what they love.

And they help out with money. You have got to put money into any church you go to, because that's what you do when you say, "Help us to help each other." That's why the band has the day.

And even today, I can't do, but they don't forget me. When you get up to ninety-something, you can't do so much. When they come to see me, they bring donations. And they say, "Well, we know how you worked in the band. . . . Here's a little donation for you." That makes me live to see another day, giving me a spirit that's good for me. So, they are helping me out. They are letting me know "I appreciate what you have done."

EIGHT

Benjamin Harrison Beckett (1927–2005)

George Washington Beckett (b. 1929)

If we give it up, what do you think the rest of them will do?

Ben:

I was born in '27, and I've been on the campground every year since then. Every single year. I was born on April 13, and I was on the campground August 13. I didn't know it, but I was there.

I haven't missed a year. George hasn't missed a year either, since he's been born. Rachel, my sister Rachel, she hasn't missed a year. We've all been there, you know. I've been on the campground every year of my life.

The first year they had me out there, it was in a covered wagon. They were farm wagons. My dad used to bring his covered wagon and walk the horses back home. If you want to stay in a wagon, you have to level the wheels; your wagon might sit one wheel higher than the other. So, they'd take a shovel and level it out below the wheels. We all stayed in there. We had to stay in there, there wasn't anywhere else to stay. We weren't going home.

They didn't do too much work during camp meeting because the farmers had laid their crops by. That means they went through their fields for the final time. They just pulled the dirt up to a row of plants with a cultivator and were done with them, then. They used to call it laying the crops by. In later fall, after camp, we used to go shuck the corn.

They didn't cook out there then. The wagons and everything just stayed there, but they would go back home; the women might have to wash some clothes, and they carried their food back all cooked. They cooked food that wouldn't spoil. I remember big baskets full of fried chicken, baked goods, ham. Fried chicken would keep for a while. Desserts, they wouldn't spoil; cakes, they made homemade cakes.

A little later, they used to have a place for eating, a makeshift dining hall. That would have been sixty years ago, roughly. They used to make them out of canvas, so they could take them right back down as soon as camp was over. They used to cook

Sitting in the grove between the bower and the wooden tents that surround it, Ben Beckett recounts memorable events in the long history of Antioch A.M.E.'s August camp meeting, in Frankford, Delaware.

out there in those big, old, black cast-iron pots. We used to call them hog-killing pots. All the people used to have them then. And when they started selling food, they made what they called chicken and dumplings in these big pots, right outside. (They did the same thing at corn-shucking gatherings.) The only vendors they had were picture-taking people, and somebody selling sheet music. Ballads, that's what they called them. They were a nickel or ten cents a piece. Maybe a man might have some snake oil. That was it. That was all.

And there used to be a big woods right in back of the campground. And those people that hung out back there—the bad crowd, I called it—did most of their gambling back there. They were gambling and drinking, too. They spent a lot of money on the inside of the grounds, buying food. They bought more food than anybody. You know how people do when they are drinking? They've got money to blow away.

George:

Our church is Antioch A.M.E., in Frankford, Delaware. The land was handed over to our church officials—my grandfather, my father, our cousins—by Old Man Phil Walls (who was a white man) or by his family to build a church. They lived across from where our church is now. According to the deed we have been able to dig up, it was always to be handed down from one generation to the next and not to be sold.

Most of the time we had camp meeting, we didn't bother with inside the church much, we would be out under the grove, with cottages in almost a complete circle facing inwards toward "the bower." We always called it the bower. That was a wood pavilion where they had service outside, outdoors, in the open air. Frankford didn't always have a bower for service, but when I was first born they had a bower.

There used to be thirty-three cottages; they are about three short now. The fronts of the cottages are toward the bower. Most of them are about twelve feet wide and about twenty-four feet going back. A lot of times they would be cut up into three rooms. My porch is about six feet wide and twelve feet long; and there's six feet for the sitting room, six feet for the bedroom, six feet for the kitchen. A hall goes from your sitting room to your kitchen, and there's a door from the hallway to the bedroom. They face inward toward the bower. People are able to sit on their porches and keep up with what is going on under the bower because they can hear—and some of them can see—what is going on.

I was probably twelve when they did away with the wagons. I guess it was probably in the thirties when they first came through with the cottages. See, the modern version of it here lately has been "cottages," but years ago, everything was called tents. And that's almost what they were, because they were very crude. They mostly had dirt floors, not wood. The fronts were sort of open. They just had a couple of sheets across the front and they opened from the center; they'd pull them back like you pull a curtain back and tie it. Most of the time there'd be a room in back where you'd do your cooking, and there'd be one room in front where the beds were. There weren't any porches, but right out front you had benches where you could sit.

After a midday cookout in the camp-meeting grove, George Beckett gives a lecture about the architecture of the cottages that surround the bower behind him.

Camp meeting has always been in August, and we had two Sundays. It always opened the second Saturday in August and closed the third Sunday. Most of the time, that's when they would be because the farmers—who were white—would allow the sharecroppers who worked for them to take a week off. (I wouldn't know of any white sharecroppers. At that time, we stayed with our race.)

Old tents such as this one at Union Wesley's campground had an open front, one room for the beds, and a half-enclosed room in the back for cooking.

We'd open up on the second Saturday of August. The first Sunday of camp was always called the big Sunday. That was when lots of people and most of the bands came down. I can never remember the camp being organized by anybody but a band, and the church working with the band. The grove would be full of people. I counted thirty-three chartered buses one time, not counting all the school buses that they had. We who had cottages were always glad to see the first weekend over, because we could take advantage of our own cottages and look forward to some relaxation.

They used to plan a few things, too. On that Monday they used to go to a place they called Strawberry Landing and have a picnic. Vacation Bible school was during that week for years. The third Sunday, like the eighteenth or the nineteenth of the month, that would be the closed-out Sunday. The closing march is on that third Sunday.

Ben:

They didn't have organized bands. They had prayer meetings, but they didn't have organized bands. Before the bands got organized, the officers of the church did most of the planning for camp meeting. But I guess the officers—the class leaders, the stewards—sang in the prayer meeting anyway. They sang in the prayer meeting. Of course, a whole lot of people used to sing in the prayer meeting. I mean just a few of them didn't. One of my grandfathers sang in the prayer meeting, but one didn't. John McCrae didn't. But Charles Beckett, my other grandfather, sang. Him, his children—my father, Edward Beckett, my uncles, and some more of them—they sang in the prayer bands. My dad used to lay on the couch at home and sing, "Don't you hear the angels singing?" That was one of his pieces. And one of his verses was

"The Lord told Thomas 'I am the man: Look at the nail prints in my hand.'" That was his verse.

They all just came out and sang together on the first Saturday night. A great big army of them. There would be *people* from other places nearby but there wouldn't be *bands* coming from anywhere else. Anybody who came would just be prayer-meeting people. They would start sometime around midnight, and then they would keep going all night long.

They sang in a circle—they didn't line up with men and women in separate rows like we do now. The leader would be in the middle, where everybody could see him and make contact with him. The people would gather around and sing they would get in the Spirit. At daybreak, they would still be singing in a circle under the grove. And they could hardly get them to stop to have the preaching on Sunday morning. The preacher would have to stop them.

16. "Don't You Hear the Angels Singing"

A Straight Hymn

The musical notation below is based on two versions of this song. One was sung by Benjamin and George Beckett of Antioch A.M.E. Church in Frankford, Delaware, on July 12, 1999, in the home of Benjamin and Mildred Beckett, in Millsboro, Delaware. The second version was sung by Condonsal Walters of Dickerson Chapel A.M.E., Millsboro, Delaware, on July 7, 1998, in the home of Elizabeth Hall, also of Millsboro.

deemed   I   don't want to be   left   be - hind -

Been   re - deemed.   Been   re -   deemed   deemed.

Return to chorus and add
verses 2 and 3, and then
repeat chorus to END.

VERSES:

2. The Lord said, "Thomas, I am the man."
"Look at the nail prints in my hand."

3. No man saw what Daniel saw.
Angel locking up the lion's jaw.

My dad said one time the preacher wanted to preach, but they couldn't stop them from singing. They even called the cops to break them up. The police couldn't break them up either. I mean, if the people are in the Spirit, what are the police going to do? They're not going to mess with it.

I remember my mother talking about how the women used to come out of the covered wagons shouting and singing. (The hymn, "Oh Mary, Oh Martha," I learned from my mother, Emily Elizabeth Beckett. I don't know where she got it, but I know where I got it.) They didn't even have time to take off their aprons, they'd be singing so. They'd forget they had their aprons on.

They all had long dresses. Aprons. The only kind of aprons they had were everyday aprons. They wore bonnets. They were different colors; they weren't matched up any kind of way. Feed-bag dresses, whatnot.

(You see, feed used to come in one-hundred-pound bags. And the material was all different kinds of designs and flowers. And they'd save the bags and they made clothes out of them. And they made *nice* clothes. And it was strong material, because it had to be strong to hold one hundred pounds of feed.)

Georgeanne Oliver might lead the closing march, but she'd take time out and sing with us children so we could sing too. (My dad and her were first cousins. Georgeanne's father, George Woolford, and my father's mother, Agnes Woolford, were brother and sister.) That wouldn't be the closing march; that would be before, maybe some weeknight. We didn't have any electric lights out there then. She took an old lantern, and she would lead us through the campground, around and between these tents, singing any one of her pieces that she used to sing. We were teeny things

17. "Oh Mary, Oh Martha"

A Straight Hymn

The musical notation below is based on a version of this song performed by the Western Shore Singing and Praying Band at Malone United Methodist in Madison, Maryland, on May 21, 1989, led by Oscar Johnson of St. Luke United Methodist of Baltimore. The song began with D below middle C as its tonic note, at a tempo of 60 quarter notes per minute. After rising in pitch and accelerating in tempo, it ended with A below middle C as its tonic, at a tempo of 130 quarter notes per minute. A and D (the third and the sixth) vary in pitch between flat and natural.

The phrase "Go tell my disciples to meet me in Galilee," which forms the crux of this lyric, was originally drawn from Matthew 28:10, but it is not uncommon in American religious folksong. It appears, for example, in the song "He Arose from the Dead," recorded by Blind Lemon Jefferson in 1927; in "John the Revelator"; and in the song "Run Along Mary."

Repeat from
beginning, add second
verse, and repeat
chorus to END.

VERSE:

2. Choose a robe and try it on.
If it fits, you can wear it home.

then. I was about eight, not much older than that. And we would think we were doing
something!

We didn't know what we were doing, but all I know is we were doing it. That's
been sixty years ago or better.

It was probably in the thirties that they did away with the wagons and came
through with the cottages. Everybody built their own tents. The first one I had
belonged to one of my distant cousins, William Walter. He was an old guy; his wife,
Molly, was related to my mother. It was an old place so, bye and bye, I tore it down
and I built another one right from the ground up.

My wife, Mildred, and I first started the one I have now; I would say this tent
is not more than six or eight years old. I put cement blocks down first and leveled
them up. So I got them all the same height. And then I went and got the sills in a
big truck. The sills are what you put down for your foundation. They went on top
of the blocks, this way, this way, this way, and this way, four sides. They are oak,
four-by-sixes, I think. And they were not long enough to go the whole length: you
put two on each side. You had to notch them out: cut a piece out of this one here,
and a piece out of the other one here, so you can put one on top of the other, so
they'd be level, the same height. Then you run your joists across every so often. Me
and Mildred put them in ourselves.

While adults talk around the outdoor dinner table, children play around a tree in the grove of Antioch's campground.

And then after she and I got it started, my brothers came and helped. Every time I turned around, they were helping. I put a thick plywood floor in next, on top of those joists. And then you nail the framing down on top of it, all the way around. I used two-by-fours. The A-frame rafters were two-by-sixes. My brother, Bill, helped put them up. And then we put on that outside siding. It's T-111 siding—that's wood, its made for exterior. It comes in four-by-eight sheets, or four-by-ten sheets, whatever you want. You put plywood on top of the rafters, and your final roofing on top of that. Then you paint it.

I did my own blueprint when I laid the tent out, and got my floor and everything in there. I marked out "I want this for my bathroom; I want this for my kitchen; I want this for my porch." I just marked out everything. Then I started putting up the inside framing, for the inside walls. I think it is fourteen by thirty-two feet. There would be the porch first, and then the sitting room (we've got a bed in there too). On the right-hand side is a hallway as you go back to the kitchen. On the left-hand

Two girls play with an outdoor
water spigot at Antioch's camp.

side as you leave the front is the bedroom. And then there is the kitchen. On the left-hand side of the kitchen is the bathroom, about five foot square.

The porch is six foot deep and fourteen feet long. The sitting room is eight feet by fourteen. The bedroom is not as big because we have got the hallway going through there; the bedroom would be about eight feet by eleven. The kitchen is somewhere around twelve by fourteen. My tent is one story: with the porch closed in, just about five rooms.

George:

This house I live in now was a camp-meeting tent. I moved it here, about a mile and a quarter from the campground. I bought the place from a distant cousin, Henry Long, who was Minerva Oliver's brother. (She was about a third cousin on my mother's side.) He was never a member of our church but he and his family came down for camp every year.

We got a man who moves houses to move it in 1949. And after I moved it here,

I tried to get loans to make a home of it. I went to two or three places. I had them come up and look at it and the man that came up—yes, he was a white guy—told me it was no good, I just ought to move it back toward the woods for a chicken house. I always thought that he did that because they didn't want to fool with repairing anything, and he wanted to build me a new house. I imagine he knew it could be repaired because it wasn't in bad shape—it was one of the better ones on the campground. But he knew I couldn't afford a new house.

It hurt my feelings, but I didn't stop. So I kept on until I got a private carpenter and I paid him to do it. That place was one room, twenty-four feet long and twelve feet wide, and instead of two stories, it was a story and a half. Upstairs, the ceilings were lower (the ceilings were low downstairs too). Over the years I expanded it.

The long side was parallel to the road. When I first remodeled it, before I ever started living in it, it went to twenty-four by twenty-four. And then, the first thing I added was a sun porch on the side, a utility room, and a bathroom, because we didn't have a bathroom downstairs. I put a washer and dryer in the utility room. And I added a garage and a family room on the other side. I moved here in 1950. It has been forty-nine years.

Ben:

Just about half of the cottages on the campground burnt down in 1943. I think about thirteen or fourteen burnt down. It burnt the church down, burnt the bower down, too.

George:

It started with the tent beside my mother's cottage. Somebody said it started in Francis McCrae's tent. The McCraes had a tent on each side of my mother. (I think Joe Henry McCrae and Francis McCrae, who were husband and wife, were first cousins to my grandfather and second cousins to my mother. Our grandfather was John McCrae. All the McCraes were related. Frankford was full of them.)

It was on our closing Sunday. A lot of the men were at Berlin's camp. It was Berlin's big Sunday. And that's where a lot of the men were when the fire started.

Ben:

Berlin, Maryland, is about sixteen miles from Frankford, going south. That's a United Methodist church. Gus Oliver was the band captain and his tent was beside mine, and they had left the children in bed that night. And you talk about when they heard the news! He had a car, so he wasn't long in coming home. But they were all right; the fire hadn't reached there. The kids were in their beds inside the tent, sleeping. My aunt—my mother's sister, Anna Jones—was sleeping, and she probably would have burnt up, but we woke her. (She was Anna McCrae until she married a guy from Berlin named Lemont Jones.)

The fire destroyed half the tents and the church and the bower. I don't know what year the second bower was built, but Mr. Will Oliver was just about the head of that. He had the get-up-and-go, along with his brother, Gussy. Once they got ready to build it, it didn't take too long.

The band has been organized for about fifty-six years this December. I forget the exact year, but the band captains, and the assistant band captain, and the women's captains, that came along about fifty some years ago. Before that they had prayer meetings but they didn't have organized bands; just whoever was around it was one big band. Fifty years ago, when the preacher preached, whoever was there just sang in the prayer meeting, from this church or that church, everybody just joined in. When they started organizing, Frankford could sing alone.

Will Oliver was the first captain. Allie Woolford was the second one. (Georgeanne Oliver and Allie Woolford, who was band captain, were brother and sister.) Gussy Oliver was the captain after Allie Woolford. Now William Harris is captain. He's 103 years old. After they got organized, they went singing more and traveling more, and they started bringing a lot more people.

William Harris, once captain of Antioch's Singing and Praying Band, stands at the back door of his tent at Antioch and celebrates over one hundred years of life with satisfaction.

George:

See, there wasn't as much traveling anywhere. Will and Gussy Oliver really started it. (Their mother and our mother, Emily Elizabeth McCrae, were related. The Mc-Craes, the Woolfords, and the Olivers were all related. That makes Gus Oliver and them related to us.) Those two brothers were the ones started building up the bands coming to Frankford, because they started going on the Western Shore, and Taylors Island, and places that people around here didn't know anything about. And the more they traveled, the more those bands started coming back to Frankford. They really built it up.

Georgeanne Oliver was the first women's captain, and Minerva Oliver was the second captain, second women's captain. (Minerva was Gussy Oliver's wife.)

Will Spicer from Philadelphia and Alexander Hall and Matthew Watts from Magothy would come here on Saturday night, the second Saturday night in August, and they sang till almost morning. (They used to hate to break up, but they had to leave to go to Hall's Methodist, in Marley Neck, because Marley Neck camp was that same day.) Spicer would always be here the first weekend with his band.

Ben:

They wouldn't start singing until midnight Saturday night, after midnight preaching. Matthew Watts from Magothy (Old Man Watts used to sing "Ain't no grave gonna hold my body in that day"), some of them from St. James in Baltimore, and the Wilmington band from Mt. Carmel used to come down here a lot then. The captain's name was Brother Scott. Charles Raymond Stanley, Sherman Wilson, and Buster Wilson from Dorchester County, Maryland—all of them would be there. The Hall men from Friendship United Methodist, off of Route 24 going toward

After ten days of tarrying on the Antioch campground, local band members close out their annual event on a Sunday evening, marching from tent to tent around the grove, singing the old song "He Put John on the Island."

Rehobeth: Fred Hall, Winfield Hall, Jake Hall, York Hall, and their wives would be down here marching the grounds like I don't know what. Those old people could do something. That would be the first Sunday.

George:

And I remember as a child waking up one morning and looking out the window and I used to see these bands marching around the camp. This was when we had really large camps. And one in particular I remember seeing was this really tall man. And he happened to be Levi Stewart. Levi was a *singing* man. I would say he and Will Spicer were the *singingest* men we ever knew.

Will Spicer would be there the first weekend with his band. But then they built it up so that he would come back again on the third Sunday, the close-out Sunday, for the closing march. He was a *singing* man. I mean he had a *terrible* voice on him. You haven't heard "I, John, Saw" unless you heard him. Oh, my dear! That was always the closing march. Ever since I can remember, it was "I, John, Saw."

Ben:

We had converts during camp. Most of the times it would be camp times for converts because that's when everybody comes, saints, sinners, everybody. Even people who didn't belong to any kind of church came to camp. Converts would come when the preacher extended the invitation, but a lot of times, the choirs, the prayer-meeting people, the preaching had already prepared the converts to come. Most of the time you get converts, the people are on one accord (if there is any discord, there

18. "He Put John on the Island"

A Straight Hymn

The musical notation presented below is based on a version of this song performed by the Eastern Shore Singing and Praying Band at Malone United Methodist in Madison, Maryland, on May 17, 1986, led by Gus Bivens. The text tells the story of John, the author of Revelation, when he was exiled on the island of Patmos. Toward the end of the hymn, the story of John is combined with that of the resurrection and anticipated second coming of Jesus.

Although this song is in leader-chorus form, everyone in the bands knows most of the verses and joins in as soon as the leader indicates the next verse he will choose. The song style, then, can be accurately described as overlapping call-and-response. Each line—comprised of one line of text and the chorus—is repeated a minimum of four times, but often eight and sometimes twelve times. As with most band hymns, it begins slowly, at 80 half notes per minute, and speeds up during the course of the performance, ending at 108 half notes per minute. While the bands begin the song in F major, the pitch rises during the performance. It thus concludes in A major. Frequently the bands begin this song in formation, with a line of men facing a line of women, a bench between them. Then they march around the bench and around the church or the campground, completing the song by forming a circle, facing the leader in the middle.

This hymn is similar to others collected early in the twentieth century. A version of it first appeared in the journal the *Southern Workman* 30, no. 11 (November 1901): 590, and in the third edition of the book *Cabin and Plantation Songs*, compiled by Thomas Fenner and published by the Hampton Institute, also in 1901. At a later date, the hymn was also published in R. N. Dett's *Religious Folk-Songs of the Negro*. A variant of the text appears on page 96 in Newman I. White's *American Negro Folk-Songs*. Finally, *The Frank C. Brown Collection of North Carolina Folklore*, edited by White, published another variation of this text (vol. 3, 604).

VERSES:

2. He put him there to starve him. I John saw.

3. He could not starve old John. I John saw.

4. The raven came and fed him. I John saw.

5. He fed him milk and honey. I John saw.

6. I heard Jesus say. I John saw.

7. I am the way. I John saw.

8. The truth and the life. I John saw.

9. He put him in the grave. I John saw.

10. He laid there three days. I John saw.

11. Third day in the morning. I John saw.

12. See the grave busted. I John saw.

13. He who was dead. I John saw.

14. Won't die no more. I John saw.

15. He's coming back again. I John saw.

16. Mary don't touch my robe. I John saw.

17. Don't let it drag in the dust. I John saw.

are no converts). Sometimes they'd shout, sometimes they'd come up running. But a lot of times, the converts would come when the preacher extended the invitation. They were just waiting for somebody to say, "Come!"

None of the churches around here had prayer meetings every Sunday. Camp meeting would be the main event of the year. During the year, it would be mostly camp times or watch-meeting nights. That was it; no other prayer meetings.

George:

Camp meeting was large for a lot of people who had nothing to do with the bands because a lot of people who lived away came home for camp. They took their vacations. And that's what made camp interesting, because there would be something going on pretty well all week. Most of these cottages were family related anyway.

We are struggling now with the [A.M.E.] Conference wanting to claim our church. Ever since we've known Antioch A.M.E., it has been *under* the conference, but it was never thought that Antioch *belonged* to the conference. We always said that if the A.M.E. Conference was to get our property, in a few years, those cottages would be torn down and they'd probably put up a highrise or senior citizens' center, with the money going right back to the conference. We wouldn't have any say about our own property, which was given to our foreparents.

Ben:

Until later years, everybody down there on the campground was related: cousins, aunts, uncles, whatnot. The Becketts have always been there and the Olivers have always been there. Charlie McCrae had a tent. Then his sister, Lena McCrae, had one. She was the McCrae boys' sister. She was Orville and Charles's sister. That's right next door to Rachel, our sister Rachel. But that used to be Francis McCrea's tent. Joe Henry and Francis McCrae, they were all those brothers' mother and father, like Virgil, John Elmer, Norman McCrae, Charles McCrae, Orville McCrae. They were related to us.

Allie Woolford's tent is three doors from mine. Georgeanne Oliver's daughter, Marg, has got it now. Mrs. Alfonzer McCrae—she married Orville McCrae—has got a tent right beside of mine. She has three children in our hand now. And Tyrone Oliver has got the old tent that Will Oliver used to have. But then I have a tent and George has a tent, my brother Bill has a tent, and my sister Rachel has a tent. Rachel's got the same spot my mother used to have, but not the same tent.

I like to stay on the campground. I just always did, all of my life. I figure, during camp time, I am supposed to stay on the campground; that's where I am supposed to sleep at and everything. You take somebody like us, if we give it up, what do you think the rest of them will do? I mean, that's not why I stay out there. *It's camp time:* I stay out there because I want to.

Epilogue

George:

I would say Miss Georgeanne was the strongest woman Antioch had. I remember the first time I heard Miss Georgeanne singing that particular piece—"If I can just make it in"—was at Magothy. When the band from Frankford was down in prayer, you would never find Miss Georgeanne down on the mourners' bench where the women bow. Rather than kneeling down she would always be over by the piano, sitting. I think it was just her style.

And Mr. Gus would say call on her to sing, saying, "*Georgeanne!*"

And I remember Georgeanne coming out with that piece. And I remember Joe Spicer from Baltimore, he'd say, "Come on, Anne, come on, Anne!"

She could really do it, too. And she had a style that was different from anybody's. It was the style she sang and the verses she sang. She'd just shake herself when she sang. "Trouble in the morning, trouble all day." I mean she just put herself right in it: "Be no trouble in that day."

She'd get it started, and Mr. Gus and them would start bringing it up. But she could do it. Miss Georgeanne could do it.

Ben:

I miss old Charles Raymond Stanley. I tell you, it really bothered me when I found out he had passed. I miss him more than anybody I ever missed before from

Clusters of singers offer each other support and love as they conclude a hymn and settle in for a prayer at Antioch's December Eastern and Western Shore Band Day.

the Eastern Shore bands. Everyone else has treated me fine, but me and Charles Stanley just hooked up together some kind of way. I don't know why.

We called one another a lot. Every time I called, he'd say, "Benny, I was just thinking about you," or, "Benny, you made my day." He always called me Benny.

There was something about him. I don't know what it was. The first time I ever met Charles Stanley was in the early fifties, at a camp meeting down at Friendship Methodist Church in Millsboro. I don't remember what he was singing, but he was on fire. He had gotten up in the Spirit, and he had left the floor and was on the church benches, walking.

I told him, I told him one time, I said, "Boy, you had lost your mind."

He was carried away; he was just out of himself. They are not like that all the time, and not all that often. But every once in a while it happens to them. Charles Stanley, he didn't walk the benches everywhere he went, but when he got going, there was no telling what he was going to do. I told him he was a crazy man. He wasn't really crazy; he was carried away.

He was a live wire wherever he went.

It seemed like Charles Stanley could just get them together down on the Eastern Shore. Seems like he could just get them together. Sherman Wilson had a bus, and a lot of times, they would get Minnie Lee or Florence Wilson to collect the fares. But Charles Stanley would load the bus to take the trip to some church meeting or camp meeting. He would know everybody who was supposed to be there, and they wouldn't pull out until he had checked them off that list he had.

Even when Charles Stanley quit singing because of his health, he still traveled with them until he couldn't go. Heart problems, short-windedness—everything was happening to him, I guess. A lot of times he would stand on the sidelines, and he would holler at me while we were singing, "*Pick 'em up, Benny; pick 'em up, Benny! Come on, Benny, pick 'em up!*"

I guess he figured I sing high.

Charles Stanley used to say, "Boy, the Eastern Shore, they are slow getting going," he said, "but once they get rolling," he said, "they *roll*."

It seems that after they got straightened out, they put that piece in overdrive. It seems like they could just drive on into it. When they got there, it was something else.

We were down at Wayman Good Hope A.M.E. on the Western Shore one Sunday and he told me *I* lost *my* mind. "Benny, you're crazy; you are going crazy," he said. "I don't want to see you like that no more."

I heard Leona Spicer from Liner's Road say, "I ain't gonna mess with him, he'll *hurt* you!" talking about me. Leona said, "I ain't gonna mess with him," because I was crazy.

You aren't *really* crazy. You let go and are not your natural self. But nobody was going to get hurt, nothing like that.

I think we were singing "We will never grow old." It seemed like all the Eastern

Shore was going crazy. Susanna Watkins was living then and she said, "Boy, this is like old times!"

And they couldn't get them loaded up on the bus to go home. They would come and get one and get him to the door to go home, and they'd tell him, "Stay there now, don't leave; we're gonna go get the rest of them."

The one they left at the door, he would go right back into the meeting. He'd be gone by the time they came back, gone back in the meeting. Well, if we didn't have a time! It was something in that place. I tell you, we didn't ever have a time like that in Wayman's before.

NINE

Gus Bivens
(1913–96)

Whatever you do right, it will be counted.

I GOT CONVERTED WHEN I WAS TWELVE YEARS OLD, in little Tindley Chapel in Pocomoke City. Dr. Tindley from Philadelphia built Tindley's Temple there. But Dr. Tindley's home was in Berlin, Maryland. I was born in 1913, but he had built Tindley Chapel—little Tindley—in Pocomoke, before I was born.

We had a gang of boys and we were in the back there, talking. Aunt Mary prayed the prayer for the reading of the scripture. Aunt Mary was an old woman, but she could pray a prayer. And she knew that Bible; no doubt about it, she knew it. *Mercy, goodness!*

I was listening. And I had made up my mind, "Not me. I'm going out of here," because it was getting hot. When she got her Spirit, it spread all over. The fire of God comes in at those times; you can't do anything about it. We went out like a light. Fell out like dead people. Yes, sir, right stiff. Just like somebody dropped you. *Boom!*

You don't see anything coming to you. You just have salvation in you. So that's how we got converted.

They had a basin of water and they came and wiped our faces with that cool water, and that brought us to. We came through shouting. "Well," I said, "this is the greatest!"

I thought I was going to beat it. I was going to run on out of there. But you can't run from the Spirit. I found that out.

I had a vision a long time ago, when I was about twenty-one years old, and backsliding. We had some boys who would go down to Public Landing near Ocean City and they would get off. And I had it in my mind that I would get off with them. So, I had been out following those boys, drinking.

My mother and father didn't like any strong drinks. So they told me that next day, "You don't do that. God gave you a good pail of milk and you just turned it over."

I said to myself, "*Lord, have mercy!*"

Then, I was driving this mule cart, going down to the woods. I started singing. I was singing.

And this voice spoke to the mules, saying, "Stop."

And he told me, "If you're going out here to sing," he said, "you sing good. And if you do it, do it right.

Graciously welcoming the Singing and Praying Bands to Shiloh United Methodist Church, in Johnson's Neck, Maryland, host captain Gus Bivens compares the bands of the past with those of today. Photograph by William M. David Jr.

"Do it right. Whatever you do right, it will be counted. You can sing and damn yourself; you can sing and make glory for yourself."

Then I went on, and I saw this vision. It was far off. And I saw him. He was giving out something like a little testament, little Bibles, and said, "Eat it and take the medicine."

And I said, "From this day forward, I am not going to follow those people. Let them go suit themselves. What I do, I'm going to do right."

Those old people were something. They had more spirit than we do. You got a lot of schooling from the older people, like Gus Oliver from Frankford, Sam Jones from Dame's Quarter. Sam Jones was something. They taught us things, hymns like: "I saw him kneeling down on the cold ground. / He was the most helpless poor creature that ever was found."

I've known that for years but it has been a long time for me to sing a give out hymn like that. A woman over here in Cambridge named Lilly Chester sang that hymn. Lilly could sing a hymn, honey. Lilly could sing any kind of hymn.

At ease in his home turf in southeastern Delaware and Maryland, lifetime band member Gus Bivens looks down with affection at a resting Alfred Green, another workhorse of the Singing and Praying Bands.

19. "I Saw Him Low Kneeling"

A Give-out Hymn

The notation of this hymn fragment is based on a version of the song sung by Gus Bivens during an interview in his home in Cambridge, Maryland, on July 23, 1987. Hymn texts similar to this appeared in print numerous times in the nineteenth century, according to the *Dictionary of American Hymnology*, first in a songbook called *Revival Melodies* (Boston, 1843). In this songbook, the hymn is called "Christ in the Garden," and it begins with the line, "When nature was sinking in stillness to rest." When the text entered into the Singing and Praying Band repertoire is unknown.

VERSES:

2. So deep was his sorrow, so fervent his prayers,
That down on his bosom rolled blood, sweat, and tears.

3. I wept to behold him, just to ask him his name,
Said: "I'm Jesus of Nazareth, from heaven I came."

4. He fled from the garden then he spread it abroad,
I ran and I shouted, "Oh, Glory to God!"

They had some pretty hymns that they used to sing, like "John baptized in the river, as he was passing by," and:

> Among them dry bones,
> Among them dry bones,
> Ezekiel prayed in the valley
> Among them dry bones.

And like that hymn that came to me in a vision:

> I'm gonna walk through the streets of the city;
> I have loved ones that's gone on before.
> I'm gonna sit down by the banks of the river;
> I'm gonna rest forever more.

The Spirit gave it to me. I was lying in there and it came right to me (they often come to me). Now I can sing that kind of hymn.

Now, see, the verses, you get them from the Bible:

> Give me the witness and told me to go,
> I'm gonna rest forever more,
> Give me the trumpet and he told me to blow,
> I'm gonna rest forever more.

Or

> This old world is coming to an end,
> I'm gonna rest forever more,
> What's gonna come of the wicked men,
> I'm gonna rest forever more.

Now these verses, you get right out of the Bible. We've done this for years: "Isaiah saw him come from the East. / Isaiah said he was the Prince of Peace." You find the verses in the Bible. The bands and local preachers studied them in the Bible. They won't be rhymed up just like that, but they're the truth! You remember Jesus was standing on the shore and saw Peter on the Sea of Galilee? He was out there in a boat. Peter spoke on the boat, and said, "If Thou art the son of the living God, bid me to come."

Jesus told him, he said, "Come Peter."

Peter started walking. And Peter was walking, doing pretty good until he looked down. Faith had gone. He looked down, and Jesus looked at Peter and said, "Oh, what little faith!" So: "Peter put on the fisherman's coat [John 21:7]. / He walked on water out the boat" [Matt. 14:28–31]. The word of what you are rhyming out is the truth!

20. "As He Was Passing By"

A Straight Hymn

The musical notation presented below is based on a rendition of this song given by Condonsal Walters during an interview at the home of Elizabeth Hall in Millsboro, Delaware, July 7, 1998. The tune to which this hymn is sung is also used to sing the straight hymn "Among Them Dry Bones."

Repeat verse, and then return to
chorus. Proceed to next verses,
and then return to chorus to END.

VERSES:

2. The Lord said, "Thomas, I am the man."
"Look at the nail prints in my hand."

3. No man saw what Daniel saw,
Angel looking up the lion's jaw.

21. "I'm Gonna Walk through the Streets of the City"

A Straight Hymn

The notation given below is based on a version of this song performed by the Eastern Shore Singing and Praying Band at Malone United Methodist Church in Madison, Maryland, on September 14, 1986, led by Gus Bivens. The song began with B below middle C as its tonic note, at a tempo of 82 quarter notes per minute. After rising in pitch and accelerating in tempo, it ended with A above middle C as its tonic, at a tempo of 172 quarter notes per minute.

The text and tune of this hymn, to which Bivens asserted authorship, are related to those of the well-known, multiversed folk hymn, "I'm going to walk through the streets of the city where my Savior has gone on before." Four-line choruses with similar themes are common in camp-meeting and gospel hymn traditions. Yet Bivens legitimately asserted that this song came to him one day when he was sleeping. The process of song creation and spirituality is subtle and ongoing, with old songs and tunes being reworked to form new ones, through the agency of the Holy Spirit.

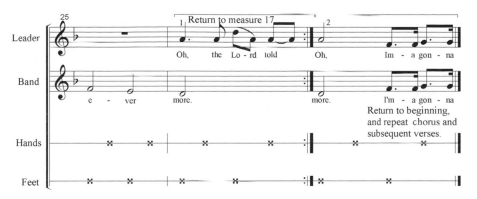

VERSES:

2. Oh, I want to meet-a-my mother that day,
When she cross the ocean way.

3. Oh, trouble in the morning, trouble all day.
(There'll) be no trouble in that day.

4 Get in the chariot, who's gonna ride?
Take-a-my Jesus by my side.

5. Passerby make way, the son's going by.
God's gonna open up the blind man's eye.

6. Hung on the cross till the sun went down.
Dead saints got up and walked around.

7. Just as busy as he can be,
One of these days he'll come after me.

Now, when we kneel at the mourners' bench, you promise the Lord, and come through, shouting all over the place. And the shepherd is your leader. So we say it like this: "I promised the Lord I'd be a good boy. / Follow the shepherd and shout for joy." Nobody rhymed that out like that but me.

We have people in the prayer meeting now that wonder why we don't get happier than we do. You know why? They fool with God's word. A lot of people think you can go out there and do whatever you want, but you can't. Also, these men don't know how to sing. They try, but they don't know what "*tarrying*" is. You *tarry* until you are endowed with the Holy Ghost. At one time, the Spirit of God wasn't given out. You had to go up to Jerusalem on the day of Pentecost and *tarry* to get the Holy Ghost. Now, you don't have to go up to Jerusalem. You can get the Holy Ghost right here. You have got to *wait* on your knees at the mourners' bench till it comes.

At one time, others would be in the back of the church, and when the Singing and Praying Band got that right key, when the band sang something that touched them within, those people would be willing to come to the mourners' bench. Now what *happens* when you are singing a hymn and everybody grabs it and it flies? There was something about it that made it happen.

See, people won't believe you, but I tell you what: we're in sin. You've got to get trash out of your mind and praise God to the highest and *then* you'll get the Holy Ghost. You can't play with God; you can't live in sin and get holy. But if you live right, you can do it. They tell you to come out from among the wicked or you just can't make it to the city.

My uncle had a hymn he always sang: "God don't want no cowardly soldiers in his band. / God only wants the valiant and hardy soldiers in his band." A lot of the men in the band today, he would have taken out (they watched you then and if you weren't going right, they would tell you about it).

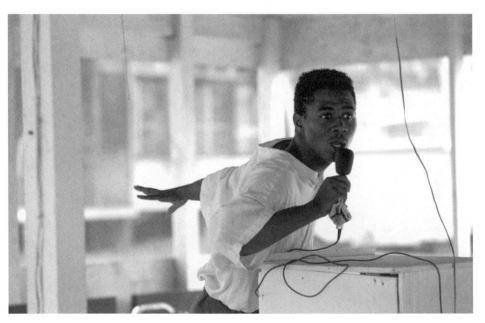

Marlon Hall preaches a lively sermon under the outdoor tabernacle on the campground of Union Wesley Church, in Clarksville, Delaware.

Seated beneath the outdoor tabernacle of Union Wesley Church, a weary Joe Spicer leans on his cane after a lifetime of laboring in the Spirit.

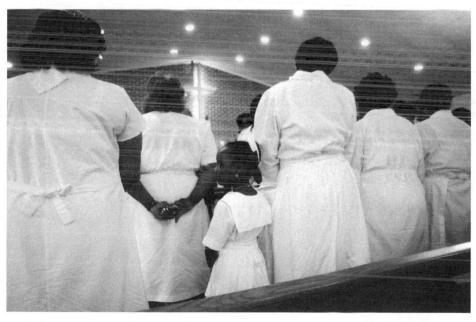

As the band sisters stand for the dedication of the offering, young Leteisha Hunt gazes off into the distance. Will the band tradition be passed along to the next generation?

And he said, "You may not go out here and do everything you can do and expect to make the journey. You can't do it: 'Be ye separated!'"

All those people you see today. I sang with their parents, their fathers and mothers, years ago when I was young. And it was solid. My mother, Laura Bivens, and my father, Norwood Bivens, both sang in the band.

I've seen them go on the campground and run every sinner off of there. They said, when they were run out, "I saw something coming up, running through me like fire and I had to go."

That was nothing but the Holy Ghost running the devil through the woods.

Now they get to singing and going on, but they don't take the *time* to sing.

Sources

Personal Interviews by the Author

Allen, Mary. June 15, 1993; March 23, 1996; June 19, September 17, November 8, 1997; January 26, 1998.

Beckett, Benjamin. April 14, May 24, 1999.

Beckett, Benjamin and George, together: August 17, 1996; July 12, October 27, November 4, 1999.

Beckett, George. May 24, 1999.

Bivens, Gus. November 13, December 30, 1986; July 23, 1987; August 4, 1996.

Colbert, Samuel Jerry. August 21, 1996; March 30, 2000; November 11, 2001; April 6, 2002.

Green, Alfred. September 3, December 22, 1995; January 3, March 9, 1996.

Johnson, Edward. November 29, 1983; May 31, June 2, 1984; May (day unknown), August 30, 1985; September 20, October 14, 1986; March 19, March 30, April 8, July 20, November 5, November 6, 1987; June 1, December 30, 1988; May 18, 1989.

Stanley, Gertrude. August 10, 1996; July 20, November 17, 1999; February 21, 2000.

Walters, Cordonsal. July 5, 1992; August 18, 1996; May 18, September 14, September 24, November 27, 1997; July 7, 1998.

Watkins, Susanna. November 18, 1992; June 28, 1993; June 16, 1996.

Recordings by the Author

Allen, Mary, hymn leader. "I'm a Soldier Bound for Glory." Eastern and Western Shore Singing and Praying Bands Service. St. Paul A.M.E. Zion Church, Salisbury, Wicomico County, Maryland. October 1996.

"All My Appointed Time." Eastern and Western Shore Singing and Praying Bands Service. Christ United Methodist Church, Baltimore City, Maryland. October 28, 1984.

Beckett, Benjamin, hymn leader. "I Heard Jesus Say." Testimony Service. Lane United Methodist Church, Taylors Island, Dorchester County, Maryland. August 1, 1999.

Beckett, Benjamin, and George Beckett. "Don't You Hear the Angels Singing." Recorded in the home of Benjamin and Mildred Beckett, Millsboro, Sussex County, Delaware. July 12, 1999.

Beckett, George. "Satisfied, My Lord, Satisfied." Recorded during a personal interview in the home of George Beckett, Frankford, Sussex County, Delaware. May 24, 1999.

Bivens, Gus, hymn leader. "He Put John on the Island." Eastern Shore Singing and Praying Band Service. Malone United Methodist Church, Madison, Dorchester County, Maryland. May 17, 1986.

————, hymn leader. "I'm Gonna Walk through the Streets of the City." Eastern Shore Singing and Praying Band Service. Malone United Methodist Church, Madison, Dorchester County, Maryland. September 14, 1986.

————. "I Saw Him Low Kneeling." Recorded in his home, Cambridge, Dorchester County, Maryland. July 23, 1987.

Colbert, Samuel Jerry, hymn leader. "There Is a Fountain Filled with Blood." Eastern and Western Shore Singing and Praying Bands Service. Jefferson United Methodist Church, Smithville, Dorchester County, Maryland. July 5, 1998.

Cromwell, James, hymn leader. "It's Jesus Christ I Long to Find." Eastern and Western Shore Singing and Praying Bands Service. Williams A.M.E. Church, Newark, Worcester County, Maryland. November 23, 1986.

Ennels, Catherine, hymn leader. "And Am I Born to Die?" Eastern Shore Singing and Praying Band Service. Asbury Town Neck United Methodist Church, Severna Park, Anne Arundel County, Maryland. July 19, 1998.

————. "We Will Never Grow Old." Eastern and Western Shore Singing and Praying Bands Service. Malone United Methodist Church, Madison, Dorchester County, Maryland. September 14, 1986.

Jennings, Wilton, hymn leader. "When Jesus Walked upon the Earth." Eastern and Western Shore Singing and Praying Bands Service. John Wesley United Methodist Church, Liner's Road, Dorchester County, Maryland. June 8, 1986.

Johnson, Edward, hymn leader. "Blow, Gabriel." Eastern Shore Singing and Praying Band Service. Coolspring United Methodist Church, Girdletree, Worcester County, Maryland. June 27, 1987.

Johnson, Oscar, hymn leader. "Oh Mary, Oh Martha." Western Shore Singing and Praying Band Service. Malone United Methodist Church, Madison, Dorchester County, Maryland. May 21, 1989.

Marine, Katherine, hymn leader. "Over on the Other Side of Jordan." Eastern Shore Singing and Praying Band Service. Lane United Methodist Church, Taylors Island, Dorchester County, Maryland. August 6, 2000.

Opher, Ralph, hymn leader. "Jesus Fed Me When I Was Hungry." Eastern Shore Singing and Praying Band Service. Friendship United Methodist Church, Millsboro, Sussex County, Delaware. October 30, 1983.

Smith, Carrie, hymn leader. "People I Used to See." Eastern and Western Shore Singing and Praying Bands Service. John Wesley United Methodist Church, Liner's Road, Dorchester County, Maryland. June 9, 1985.

Stanley, Gertrude, prayer-giver. Eastern Shore Singing and Praying Band Service. St. Paul's United Methodist Church, Harrisville, Dorchester County, Maryland. August 17, 1986.

Walters, Cordonsal. "As He Was Passing By." Recorded in the home of Elizabeth Hall, Millsboro, Sussex County, Delaware. July 7, 1998.

————. "Don't You Hear the Angels Singing." Recorded during a personal interview in the home of Elizabeth Hall, Millsboro, Sussex County, Delaware. July 7, 1998.

————. "March Along." Recorded during a personal interview in the home of Elizabeth Hall, Millsboro, Sussex County, Delaware. July 7, 1998.

White, Bernard, prayer-giver. Western Shore Singing and Praying Band Service. Friendship United Methodist Church, Millsboro, Sussex County, Delaware. October 30, 1983.

————, prayer-giver. Western Shore Singing and Praying Band Service. Jefferson United Methodist Church, Smithville, Dorchester County, Maryland. June 30, 1985.

————, prayer-giver. Western Shore Singing and Praying Band Service. St. Paul's United Methodist Church, Harrisville, Dorchester County, Maryland. August 17, 1986.

Works Cited

Allen, Richard. *The Life Experience and Gospel Labors of the Rt. Rev. Richard Allen.* 1833; rpt., Nashville, Tenn.: Abingdon Press, 1969.

Allen, William Francis. "The Negro Dialect." *The Nation*, December 14, 1865, 744–45.

Allen, William Francis, Charles P. Ware, and Lucy McKim Garrison. *Slave Songs of the United States.* New York: Peter Smith, 1867.

Bennett, William W. *Memorials of Methodism in Virginia.* Richmond, Va.: n.p., 1870.

Berlin, Ira. *Slaves without Masters: The Free Negro in the Antebellum South.* New York: Pantheon, 1974.

Blackham, Harold John. *Six Existentialist Thinkers.* New York: Harper and Row, 1959.

Brackett, Jeffrey. *The Negro in Maryland.* 1889; rpt., New York: Negro Universities Press, 1969.

Bradford, Sarah H. *Harriet Tubman: The Moses of Her People.* 1869; rpt., Secaucus, N.J.: Citadel, 1961.

Bruce, Dickson D., Jr. *And They All Sang Hallelujah: Plain-Folk Camp-Meeting Religion, 1800–1845.* Knoxville: University of Tennessee Press, 1973.

Carawan, Guy. "Spiritual Singing in the South Carolina Sea Islands." Report in the Highlander Folk School Mss. Records Collection. Tennessee State Library and Archives, Nashville, 1959.

Chevalier, Michel. *Society, Manners, and Politics in the United States: Being a Series of Letters from North America.* Trans. T. G. Bradford. 1839; rpt., Gloucester, Mass.: Peter Smith, 1967.

Christiansen, Abigail M. H. "Spirituals and 'Shouts' of Southern Negroes." *Journal of American Folklore* 7 (1894): 154–55.

Colbert, William. "Journal of William Colbert, 1790–1833." 13 manuscript volumes. Garrett Biblical Institute, Evanston, Ill. (Typescript available at Methodist Archives Library, St. George's United Methodist Church, Philadelphia.)

Cone, James. *The Spirituals and the Blues: An Interpretation.* San Francisco: Harper and Row, 1972.

Courlander, Harold. *Negro Folk Music U.S.A.* New York: Columbia University Press, 1963.

Curtin, Phillip. *The Atlantic Slave Trade: A Census.* Madison: University of Wisconsin Press, 1969.

David, Jonathan C. "On One Accord: Community, Musicality, and Spirit among the Singing and Praying Bands of Tidewater Maryland and Delaware." Ph.D. diss., University of Pennsylvania, 1994.

———. "On One Accord: Theology and Iconography of a Ring Shout." Paper presented at conference of the American Folklore Society, Albuquerque, New Mexico, Oct. 23, 1988.

———. "The Sermon and the Shout: A History of the Singing and Praying Bands of Maryland and Delaware." *Southern Folklore* 51 (1994): 241–63.

Dett, R. N. *Religious Folk-Songs of the Negro.* Hampton, Va.: Hampton Institute, 1927.

Douglass, Frederick. *My Bondage and My Freedom.* 1855; rpt., Urbana: University of Illinois Press, 1987.

DuBois, W. E. B., ed. *Economic Co-operation among Negro Americans.* Atlanta, Ga., Atlanta University Press, 1907.

———, ed. *The Negro Church.* Atlanta, Ga.: Atlanta Universities Press, 1903.

———. *The Philadelphia Negro: A Social Study.* 1899; rpt., Philadelphia: University of Pennsylvania Press, 1996.

Dunham, Katherine. "The Negro Dance." In *The Negro Caravan: Writings by American Negroes*, edited by Sterling A. Brown, Arthur Davis, and Ulysses Lee, 990–1000. New York: Dryden Press, 1941.

Ellinwood, Leonard, ed. *Dictionary of American Hymnology.* Fort George Station, N.Y.: University Music Editions, 1983.

"An Englishman in South Carolina: Dec 1860 and July 1862, pt. II." *Continental Monthly* 3 (January 1863): 110–17.

Epstein, Dena J. *Sinful Tunes and Spirituals: Black Folk Music to the Civil War.* Urbana: University of Illinois Press, 1977.

Fenner, Thomas, comp. *Cabin and Plantation Songs: As Sung by the Hampton Students.* Arranged by Thomas P. Fenner, Frederick G. Rathbun, and Bessie Cleaveland. 3rd ed. 1901; rpt., New York: AMS Press, 1977.

Forten, Charlotte. "Life on the Sea Islands." *Atlantic Monthly,* May 1864, 587–96.

Genovese, Eugene. *Roll, Jordan, Roll: The World the Slaves Made.* New York: Pantheon, 1972.

Georgia Writers Project of the Works Progress Administration. *Drums and Shadows: Survival Studies among the Georgia Coastal Negroes.* 1940; rpt., Athens: University of Georgia Press, 1986.

Gordon, Robert Winslow. "Folk Songs of America: Negro Shouts." *New York Times Magazine,* April 24, 1927, 4, 22.

Gutman, Herbert. *The Black Family in Slavery and Freedom, 1750–1925.* New York: Vintage, 1976.

Hale, Edward, and William C. Gannett. "The Freedmen of Port Royal." *North American Review* 101 (July 1865): 1–28.

Hawes, Bess Lomax, and Bessie Jones. *Step It Down: Games, Plays, Songs, and Stories from the Afro-American Heritage.* 1972; rpt., Athens: University of Georgia Press, 1987.

Herskovits, Melville. *The Myth of the Negro Past.* Boston: Beacon Press, 1941.

Higginson, Thomas. *Army Life in a Black Regiment.* 1870; rpt., Williamstown, Mass: Corner House Publications, 1971.

———. "Negro Spirituals." *Atlantic Monthly,* June 1867, 685–94.

Hughes, Langston, and Arna Bontemps. *Book of Negro Folklore.* New York: Dodd, Mead, 1958.

Hurston, Zora Neale. *Jonah's Gourd Vine.* 1934; rpt., New York: Harper and Row, 1990.

Husserl, Edmund. *The Idea of Phenomenology.* Trans. William P. Alston and George Nakhnakian. The Hague: Nijhoff, 1964.

Jackson, George Pullen. *Spiritual Folk-songs of Early America.* 1937; rpt., New York: Dover, 1964.

Johnson, Charles A. *The Frontier Camp Meeting: Religion's Harvest Time.* Dallas: Southern Methodist University Press, 1985.

Johnson, James Weldon, and J. Rosamond Johnson, eds. *The Books of American Negro Spirituals.* 1925; rpt., New York: Da Capo, 1977.

Jones, Charles Colcock. *The Religious Instruction of the Negroes.* 1842; rpt., New York: Negro Universities Press, 1969.

Kephart, I. L. *Biography of Jacob Smith Kessler, of the Church of the United Brethren in Christ, Compiled from His Autobiography.* Dayton, Ohio: W. J. Shuey, Publishing Agent, 1867.

Knapp, Elder Jacob, ed. *Revival Melodies, or Songs of Zion.* Boston: John Putnam, 1942.

Lee, Jesse. *A Short History of the Methodists in the United States of America, Beginning in 1766 and Continued Till 1809.* Baltimore: n.p., 1810.

Leedom, B. J. *Westtown under the Old and New Regime by Auld Lang Syne.* Wurtzburg: n.p., 1883.

Lomax, John A., and Alan Lomax. *Folksong U.S.A.* New York: Duell, Sloan, and Pearce, 1947.

Long, John Dixon. *Pictures of Slavery in Church and State.* 1857; rpt., New York: Negro Universities Press, 1969.

Lyell, Charles. *A Second Visit to the United States of North America*. New York: Harper, 1849.

"Magazine for June." *The Nation*, May 30, 1867, 432–33.

Minutes of the Methodist Conferences Annually Held in America, from 1773–1813, Inclusive. 1813; rpt., Swainsboro, Ga.: Magnolia Press, 1983.

M.R.S. "A Visitor's Account of Our Sea Island Schools." *Pennsylvania Freedman's Bulletin* (October 1866): 5–7.

Mullin, Gerald. *Flight and Rebellion*. New York: Oxford University Press, 1972.

"Negro Dances in Arkansas." *Journal of American Folk-Lore* 1 (1888): 83

Odum, Howard, and Guy Johnson. *The Negro and His Songs: A Study of Typical Negro Songs in the South*. Chapel Hill: University of North Carolina Press, 1925.

Parrish, Lydia. *Slave Songs of the Georgia Sea Islands*. New York: Creative Age Press, 1942.

Payne, Daniel Alexander. *Recollections of Seventy Years*. 1886; rpt., New York: Arno, 1969.

"Put John on de Islan'." *Southern Workman* 30, no. 11 (November 1901): 590.

Raboteau, Albert. *Fire in the Bones*. Boston: Beacon Press, 1995.

———. *Slave Religion: The Invisible Institution in the Antebellum South*. New York: Oxford University Press, 1978.

Rawick, George P., ed. *The American Slave: A Composite Autobiography*. Vols. 4, 5. Westport, Conn.: Greenwood, 1977.

Rose, Willie Lee. *Rehearsal for Reconstruction: The Port Royal Experiment*. New York: Bobbs-Merrill, 1964.

Rosenbaum, Art. *Shout Because You're Free: The African American Ring Shout Tradition in Coastal Georgia*. Athens: University of Georgia Press, 1998.

Sessions, Gene. "Camp Meeting at Willow Tree, 1881." *Journal of American Folklore* 87 (1974): 361–64.

The Song Book of the Salvation Army: The American Edition. Verona, N.J.: Salvation Army National Headquarters, 1987.

Songs of Zion. Supplemental Worship Resources 12. Nashville, Tenn.: Abingdon Press, 1981.

Spaulding, Henry George. "Under the Palmetto." *Continental Monthly* 4 (August 1863): 188–203.

Spencer, Jon Michael. *Protest and Praise: Sacred Music of Black Religion*. Minneapolis: Fortress, 1990.

Steward, Rev. T. G. *Fifty Years in the Gospel Ministry, from 1864–1914*. Philadelphia: n.p., 1914, 1921.

Stuckey, Sterling. *Slave Culture: Nationalist Theory and the Foundations of Black America*. New York: Oxford University Press, 1987.

Stumpf, Samuel Enoch. *Socrates to Sartre: A History of Philosophy*. New York: McGraw-Hill, 1966.

Thompson, Robert Farris. *African Art in Motion*. Los Angeles: University of California Press, 1972.

———. *Flash of the Spirit: African and Afro-American Art and Philosophy*. New York: Vintage, 1984.

Thorpe, Margaret Newbold. "Life in Virginia (by a Yankee Teacher)." Ms., 1907. Special Collections Division, College of William and Mary, Williamsburg, Va.

Todd, Rev. Robert W. *Methodism of the Peninsula; or Sketches of Notable Characters and Events in the History of Methodism in the Maryland and Delaware Peninsula*. Philadelphia: Methodist Episcopal Reading Rooms, 1886.

Towne, Laura. *Letters and Diary of Laura M. Towne, Written from the Islands of South Carolina, 1862–1884*. Edited by Rupert Sargeant Holland. 1912; rpt., Cambridge, Mass.: Riverside, 1969.

United States Bureau of the Census. *Negro Population in the United States, 1790–1915.* 1918; rpt., New York: Arno, 1968.

Watson, John Fanning. *Annals of Philadelphia, Being a Collection of Memoirs, Anecdotes and Incidents of the City and Its Inhabitants from the Day of the Pilgrim Founders.* Philadelphia: E. L. Carey and A. Hart, 1830.

———. *Methodist Error: Or Friendly, Christian Advise, To Those Methodists, Who indulge in Extravagant Religious Emotions and Bodily Exercises.* Trenton: D. and E. Fenton, 1819.

Wesley, John. "Rules of the Band Societies." In *The Works of John Wesley,* edited by Rupert Davies, vol. 9, 77–79. Nashville: Abingdon Press, 1989.

White, Newman I. *American Negro Folk-Songs.* 1928; rpt., Hatboro, Pa.: Folklore Associates, 1965.

———, general editor. *The Frank C. Brown Collection of North Carolina Folklore: The Folklore of North Carolina, Vol. I-VII.* Durham, N.C.: Duke University Press, 1952–64.

Williams, Marion. "The Man I'm Looking For." *I've Come So Far.* Spirit Feel Records 1002, 1986.

Williams, William Henry. *The Garden of American Methodism: The Delmarva Peninsula, 1769–1820.* Wilmington, Del.: Scholarly Resources, 1984.

Yoder, Don. *Pennsylvania Spirituals.* Lancaster Pa.: Pennsylvania Folklife Society, 1961.

———. "Toward a Definition of Folk Religion." *Western Folklore* 33, no. 1 (January 1974): 2–15.

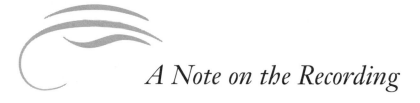

A Note on the Recording

1. Give-out hymn: "On Jordan's Stormy Banks I Stand," led by Sheila Taliaferro, of Mt. Zion United Methodist Church, at Lane United Methodist Church, Taylors Island, August 6, 2001.

> On Jordan's stormy banks I stand, and cast a wistful eye
> To Canaan's fair and happy land, where my possession lies.
>
> All over those wide extended plains shines one eternal day;
> There God the Son forever reigns and scatters night away.
>
> No chilling winds nor poisonous breath can reach that healthful shore;
> Sickness and sorrow, pain and death are felt and feared no more.
>
> When shall I reach that happy place, and be forever blest?
> When shall I see my Father's face, and in his bosom rest?
>
> Oh weeping friend don't weep for me, while standing around my bed;
> I know the way to Galilee thank God I have no dread.

2. Prayer: Bernard White, of Wayman Good Hope A.M.E. Church in Severna Park, Maryland, praying at St. Paul's United Methodist, Harrisville, Maryland, August 17, 1986.

> I am a wayward traveler here below.
> I am bound for the kingdom land.
> My master called me years ago
> When I could hardly stand.
>
> And Old Satan kept me bound in sin
> Until to God I cried.
> We'll live together here again,
> My Lord, my Lord and I.

Sometimes I feel discouraged yet,
and he comes to my relief.
And he tells me "I am he
Who died to Calvary."

And when on earth my task is done
I'll answer bye and bye.
We'll shout together again,
My Lord, my Lord and I.

He wants me now
To go and tell
The story of the cross,
How the loving father gave
His son to save the lost.

And, oh then, how he worked both night and day,
Until at last he died.
We'll travel along together again,
My Lord, my Lord and I.

Eternal God, our father, we have come once again unto thee, just as humble as we know how, with nothing to be recommended unto you but a sinful heart, a body that is much corrupted, and a mind that is prone to wander, so far from thee. We come this afternoon, our father, leaning and dependent on you, because we realize this evening that our help comes from thee, and thee alone.

We found out a long time ago, our father, that our arms is much too short, and our power is too weak to pull salvation near. We are praying that you might come this evening, our father, over the hills and the mountains, bringing free grace in one hand, bring pardon in the other, and bind up these wounds, that sin has caused all over the land.

We're praying this evening, our father, that you might hear our prayer. Bless our needy souls. Front and fight our every battle. And then, this evening, our father, we're praying for those who we are duty bound to pray for, those on their bed of affliction, those that are unable to turn over this evening, because of aching limbs, those, my father, whose hearts are out of rhythm, whose temperatures is much too high. We're praying, my father, that you might bring them a measure of comfort in knowing that you is God, that you is a doctor who's never lost a patient.

We're praying this afternoon, our father, for those who they have left behind; we pray that you might give them the strength which will be able to withstand the beating and the shifting of the winds of time of this old life here below. We're praying this evening, our father, that you might go with us, as we go through the valley of the shadow of death. We're praying, my father, that you might prepare a table before us in the presence of our enemies.

We're praying this evening, our father, for this church and people, praying for them in a special manner. Please God, lead, guide, and direct us, in the paths that you would have us to go. We're praying too, our father, that if to the right or the left we should stray, leave us not comfortless, but guide us into the way of everlasting peace. And help us this evening to help each other, each other's cross to bear. Let each his friendly aid afford and feel our brothers' care.

Bless the band people this evening, the bands who keep us together. You knows all about us, Lord. So many say we're dying out; the bands are coming to an end. I don't know, my father. I know that you is a God who is able. And you said through your written word that if we refuse to speak that the rocks would cry out. Lord, I don't want no rocks crying for me. I want you to give me the strength to go on and live so that men and women might see the good works that glorify the father who is in heaven, and that somebody down the line might see these good works, and come crying and suffering and are due to be saved. This evening, our father, our prayers this evening, the blessings thou hast showered upon us.

And when the war of life is all over, we have come to the end of our journey, give us a home in thy kingdom where thy name shall have all the praise. These blessings we ask in the name of your only son, Jesus, for his sake. My soul says, "Amen. Amen. Amen."

3. Straight hymn: "I'm Gonna Walk through the Streets of the City." Gus Bivens, leading the Eastern Shore Singing and Praying Band at Malone United Methodist Church, Madison, Maryland, September 14, 1986.

> Chorus: I'm gonna walk through the streets of the city (of the city)
> With my loved ones gone on before (on before).
> I'm gonna sit down by the banks of the river (of the river)
> I'm gonna rest forever more

1. Oh, the lord told Peter to wait and see
He that dippest out the dish with me.

2. Oh, I want to meet-a-my mother that day.
When we cross the ocean way

3. Oh, trouble in the morning, trouble all day.
(There'll) be no trouble in that day

4. [The lyrics of this verse are unclear.]

5. Get in the chariot, who's gonna ride?
Take-a-my Jesus by my side.

6. [The lyrics of this verse are unclear.]

7. Hung on the cross till the sun went down.
The dead saints got up and walked around.

8. Just as busy as he can be.
One of these days he'll come after me.

4. Prayer: Gertrude Stanley, of St. Paul's United Methodist Church in Harrisville, Maryland, praying at a band day at Antioch A.M.E. Church, Frankford, Delaware, December 12, 1999.

> On that bright eternal morning,
> God shall wipe all tears away.
> Won't that be a glorious time?
> No more sickness.
> No more sorrow.
> No more pain.
> No more death.
> On that bright eternal morning,
> God shall wipe all tears away.

Oh we thank you, Lord. We thank you, Lord. We thank you, Lord, for waking us this morning, giving us a brand new day. We just thank you, Lord. You came into our room. You sent your guardian angel who touched us with your finger of love and our eyes came open into a brand new day. It was a day that we had never seen before. But we just say "Thank you."

Oh, you've been good to us. You've been good to us, Lord. We've been traveling up and down the dangerous highways. This is our last stop. This is our last stop. We thank you this afternoon that you have been with us. You have guided us. You have protected us. You've landed us safely from time to time in our destination. For that we say "Thank you." Oh, you've been our guide and our protection all down through the years. You've been so good to us. You've brought us, Lord, through dangers seen and unseen.

This afternoon we've come before you as empty pitchers to the well to be fulfilled. Oh, fill us, Lord, with your Spirit. Fill us, Lord, with your Spirit. Teach us, Lord, just how to pray and teach us what to pray for.

Sometimes we are up and sometimes we are down. Sometimes we are almost level to the ground. But this afternoon our souls . . . we are climbing Jacob's ladder. We are climbing round by round. Every round gets higher and higher. We are soldiers of the cross.

Oh, I thank you, Lord. I thank you, Lord. You have been so good to me. You have brought me. You have kept me. There were times I could not see sky nor shore. But you came to me Lord. You said, ". . . I'm not. You don't have nothing to worry about. For I said, 'Into me you must put your trust, and I'll never leave you and I'll never forsake you.'"

And I'm standing on your promise, Lord. And I'm standing on the promises of Christ my savior. I know this afternoon that he'll never leave me and he'll never forsake me. Oh, teach us, Lord, teach us, Lord, just how to pray.

Oh, when I've gone the last mile of the way. I shall rest at the close of the day. I know. I know this afternoon. I know this afternoon. I know this afternoon without a doubt. If I live right, if I shall die right, I know this afternoon that its joy that awaits me when I've gone the last mile of the way.

I'm gonna walk through the streets of the city with my loved ones that's gone on before. I'm gonna sit down by the banks of the river. I'm gonna bathe my weary soul—for I'm weary down here—I'm gonna bathe my weary soul in the seas of heavenly rest. Not a wave of trouble is gonna roll across my peaceful breast. I'm gonna sit down by the banks of the river. There will be no more sickness. There'll be no more sorrow. There'll be no more pain. There will be no more death. Every day will be Sunday. Sabbath will have no end. I want to see mother, father, sisters, and brothers. But above all I want to see Jesus, the one who died for me, the one who set me free. Oh, everyday will be Sunday. Sabbath is gonna have no end.

These and all other blessings I ask in your name, and for your sake. My prayer says "Amen." You say not for a long prayer, so many fine words. But this afternoon the race is to him or to her that endurest to the end. The very same shall be saved. Amen.

Lord, this is our last trip. This is our last trip. We want to praise God from whom all blessings flow. Praise him all creatures here below. Praise him above the heavenly host. Praise Father, Son, and Holy Ghost. Hallelujah. Praise the Lord.

5. Straight hymn: "Job Say." Joe Spicer, of Christ United Methodist in Baltimore, leading the Eastern and Western Shore Singing and Praying Bands at a camp meeting at Lane United Methodist, Taylors Island, Maryland, August 2, 1998.

Chorus: Job say, "The Lord giveth."
　　　Job say, "(He) taketh away.
　　　Blessed be the name of the Lord."

1. Trim up you lamps and set them on the wall.
Judgment Day will soon be called.

2. Listen, oh listen, don't you hear the news?
Must be the rumbling of the horses' shoes.

3 Must I be to judgment brought
(for) Every vain and idle thought?

4. Old Job's coffin hung in the air.
Old Job's body must be there.

5. I feel my weakness every day
Weakness tells me I must go away.

6. Give me a little time, I'll talk it out right.
(I'll) Tell you about the coming of Jesus Christ.

7. I fell on my knees to say my prayers
(When) Satan come creeping up the winding stairs.

8. This campground I know quite well.
This campground I bid farewell.

Index

JONATHAN C. DAVID is an independent scholar living in Philadelphia. He has degrees from the University of Pennsylvania
in South Asia studies and in folklore and folklife.

RICHARD HOLLOWAY is a professional photographer based in
Philadelphia, where he has also done carpentry and millwork.

Music in American Life

Only a Miner: Studies in Recorded Coal-Mining Songs *Archie Green*
Great Day Coming: Folk Music and the American Left *R. Serge Denisoff*
John Philip Sousa: A Descriptive Catalog of His Works *Paul E. Bierley*
The Hell-Bound Train: A Cowboy Songbook *Glenn Ohrlin*
Oh, Didn't He Ramble: The Life Story of Lee Collins, as Told to Mary Collins *Edited by Frank J. Gillis and John W. Miner*
American Labor Songs of the Nineteenth Century *Philip S. Foner*
Stars of Country Music: Uncle Dave Macon to Johnny Rodriguez *Edited by Bill C. Malone and Judith McCulloh*
Git Along, Little Dogies: Songs and Songmakers of the American West *John I. White*
A Texas-Mexican *Cancionero:* Folksongs of the Lower Border *Américo Paredes*
San Antonio Rose: The Life and Music of Bob Wills *Charles R. Townsend*
Early Downhome Blues: A Musical and Cultural Analysis *Jeff Todd Titon*
An Ives Celebration: Papers and Panels of the Charles Ives Centennial Festival-Conference *Edited by H. Wiley Hitchcock and Vivian Perlis*
Sinful Tunes and Spirituals: Black Folk Music to the Civil War *Dena J. Epstein*
Joe Scott, the Woodsman-Songmaker *Edward D. Ives*
Jimmie Rodgers: The Life and Times of America's Blue Yodeler *Nolan Porterfield*
Early American Music Engraving and Printing: A History of Music Publishing in America from 1787 to 1825, with Commentary on Earlier and Later Practices *Richard J. Wolfe*
Sing a Sad Song: The Life of Hank Williams *Roger M. Williams*
Long Steel Rail: The Railroad in American Folksong *Norm Cohen*
Resources of American Music History: A Directory of Source Materials from Colonial Times to World War II *D. W. Krummel, Jean Geil, Doris J. Dyen, and Deane L. Root*
Tenement Songs: The Popular Music of the Jewish Immigrants *Mark Slobin*
Ozark Folksongs *Vance Randolph; edited and abridged by Norm Cohen*
Oscar Sonneck and American Music *Edited by William Lichtenwanger*
Bluegrass Breakdown: The Making of the Old Southern Sound *Robert Cantwell*
Bluegrass: A History *Neil V. Rosenberg*
Music at the White House: A History of the American Spirit *Elise K. Kirk*
Red River Blues: The Blues Tradition in the Southeast *Bruce Bastin*
Good Friends and Bad Enemies: Robert Winslow Gordon and the Study of American Folksong *Debora Kodish*
Fiddlin' Georgia Crazy: Fiddlin' John Carson, His Real World, and the World of His Songs *Gene Wiggins*
America's Music: From the Pilgrims to the Present (rev. 3d ed.) *Gilbert Chase*
Secular Music in Colonial Annapolis: The Tuesday Club, 1745–56 *John Barry Talley*
Bibliographical Handbook of American Music *D. W. Krummel*
Goin' to Kansas City *Nathan W. Pearson, Jr.*
"Susanna," "Jeanie," and "The Old Folks at Home": The Songs of Stephen C. Foster from His Time to Ours (2d ed.) *William W. Austin*
Songprints: The Musical Experience of Five Shoshone Women *Judith Vander*
"Happy in the Service of the Lord": Afro-American Gospel Quartets in Memphis *Kip Lornell*

The University of Illinois Press
is a founding member of the
Association of American University Presses.

_____

Composed in 10/13 Janson Text
by Jim Proefrock
at the University of Illinois Press
Designed by Paula Newcomb
Manufactured by Sheridan Books, Inc.

University of Illinois Press
1325 South Oak Street
Champaign, IL 61820-6903
www.press.uillinois.edu